What I Learned in My First Hundred Years

*An Inspirational Memoir:
Thriving Faithfully Through Adversity*

Nova Vaughn and Mevanee Parmer

©2024 by Mevanee Parmer
All rights reserved.

Scripture quotations used are from
the New International Version 2011,
or the Holman Christian Standard Bible 2009,
used with permission.

Steven Arias designed the book cover.

Nova's quips are not her original creations. She mentally stores away humorous anecdotes, sayings, and responses. She shares the zingers with flawless timing, even as she nears 100 years.

ISBN-13: 9798432177858

Nova's Dedication: To My Mother, Alta Wilson Wyly

I have always wished I were as wise and industrious as my mother. At ninety-nine, I am still striving for that. Mama loved God and loved Scripture. She walked with Him and led all seven of us children through the Depression and the Dust Bowl into lives of faith.

Dedicated to my mother, Nova Alta Wyly Purdy Vaughn

Capturing my mother's faith and grace has been a challenge. She continually credits God for her strength and blessings, yet she is slow to assign His hand to any particular circumstance. Her journals contain her very specific daily prayer requests.

She is as quick to pray at 99 as throughout her life. If you are holding this book, she has, most likely, prayed for you. She still says, "We need to hold on tight. "

This book grew from Nova's 2010 presentations to the Women's Council of the Amarillo Chamber of Commerce and later to Amarillo Central Church of Christ Women of the Word. She gave two thirty-minute presentations, and as we chatted, she shared more memories.

I wanted to reveal my mother's sweet spirit: her love, humor, compassion, and unclouded vision of what God desires her to be. Just as photographs capture only a moment but not a person's true beauty, these words are a snapshot of her thinking and experiences.

During her deepest trials, she held onto faithful thoughts and kind deeds. And God, who walked with her, blessed her abundantly even as she faced injury and betrayal. I witnessed her redemption as her daughter and later as her friend.

I pray that her life of faith will assure and bless you as you read, especially those walking through tides of unceasing sorrow.

Nova, at almost 100, is an encouraging, sweet soul who fears the Lord. Her children call her blessed. She has always been God's gift to us.

Table of Contents

A Word to My Grandchildren
Page 2

Lesson 1
You can exercise self-control
and sacrifice your own feelings of self-pity,
and even grief,
for the greater good.
Page 5

Lesson 2
Practice being unafraid
and trust others to step up
to their responsibilities.
Page 21

Lesson 3
Children are not pets,
but real people
who are going to have to make their own way
in the real world.
Page 35

Lesson 4
With a positive attitude and hard work,
you can do about anything
with almost nothing,
and have a good time doing it.
Page 49

Lesson 5
When you are down, get up
and begin to put one foot
in front of the other.
Page 57

Lesson 6
I learned in Africa
that we are very wealthy and privileged in this country,
full of opportunities.
Page 75

Lesson 7
Be a little venturesome,
and enjoy your whole life!
Page 86

Epilogue
Page 102

A Tribute to Ken Vaughn
From Dell Purdy
Page 112

Acknowledgments
Page 119

A Word to My Grandchildren
From Nova, aka Mom, Grandma, G.G.

I wish I could take you back to the world where I grew up, just for a week or two. I think it would help you appreciate the blessings you enjoy daily and make you less likely to complain about light and momentary inconveniences or slights.

I wish you could . . .
- hear the alarm clock or Mama's voice early in the morning bidding you to get up, to go out and milk the cows, and slop the pigs.
- stop on the way to the barn at the outdoor toilet (which would not be heated or cooled).
- return to the house and carefully pour the milk through the creamer to separate it from the cream.
- sit at the table with the family, eight in all, eating oatmeal, eggs, bacon, and biscuits for breakfast, with fresh cream or milk.
- hurry and change into one of two sets of your nice school clothes.
- stand on the back porch to brush your teeth, using baking soda for toothpaste and a glass of water for rinsing. Yes, the concrete is cold on the porch and in the house!
- rush off to catch the school bus with your lunch pail, containing two biscuits and pumpkin butter.
- just once, sit through a dust storm and sleep under a wet sheet draped over the bedposts to protect your lungs from dirt.
- help carry the wash to the old Maytag under the tree in springtime, carry water to fill its tubs, and push the clothes through the wringer four or five times before hanging them out on the line to dry.

We children enjoyed many things I wish you had in your world. So much of my growing up put me in touch with simple pleasures and nature.

I wish you could . . .

- ride the zip-line from the top of the windmill to the post pounded into the soft red dirt of the garden.
- play hide-and-seek or jump rope after the evening chores are done as the sun sets gloriously on the far horizon.
- play jacks, carrom, or checkers by lamplight.
- hear the whir of the windmill on a balmy night.
- count the songs of the mockingbird as you fall asleep.
- step out your back door and see the Milky Way and all the stars.
- stand amazed by the mysterious colored lights that sometimes appear in the northern sky.
- hop barefoot into a red ant bed, holding your breath to see if they bite.
- spend an evening helping your brothers pour water down a critter's hole to see what emerges.
- stop and listen to the chirps of the cricket behind the water shelf.
- swim in the draw after a rain.
- take in a stray animal like our old horse named Sparkplug. Like a movable diving board, he let us jump off his back in the middle of the draw.

These are my wishes, dear children, for you.

The children of Jim and Alta in a photograph from 1925: Wilson, my oldest brother, and Myrtice, my only sister, are behind. In front are Porter, me, and Bob. Two more sons, Elton and Duane, were born in 1927 and 1930. We all lost our Papa Jim in 1929, about four years after this picture was taken.

Lesson 1

**You can exercise self-control
and sacrifice your own feelings of self-pity,
and even grief,
for a greater good.**

I am a miracle emerging through the blown sand of the Dust Bowl, as are all my brothers and sister. My mother's faith and love led us safely through those difficult years. I gladly share my life, which has not always been easy, and more importantly, my faith.

By the time I was 10, I had survived three tragic disasters. God graciously packed my life with lessons. It began with Mama, Alta Wilson Wyly, a woman who inadvertently led a remarkably faithful life.

She did not choose her tragedies but carefully chose her steps through impossible circumstances. Only when I saw Ken Burns' *The Dust Bowl* documentary, did I understand more fully the miracle of her life. That disaster drove many in the Panhandle to desperation.

My mother was a loving wife and then a widow. Through all of this, she kept her loving spirit as our mother. After we lost my father, she became the farming guide for my older brother. She served on the school board, joined the Home Demonstration Club, and bought more land.

Bear with me, reader. If you've read *Keep on the Sunny Side*, a family memoir collected by my daughter, Mevanee, you may be able to skip through this first chapter. I'll add my thoughts about these events that shaped our family.

Mama was born in 1893 to Tom and Lula Wilson. Her childhood was not easy, but her parents were stable and kind. They were among the earliest settlers of Floyd County, Texas.

My older siblings and I were born near her early home. I arrived in 1924. When I was three, my family moved from that farm near Lockney, Texas, to a half-section of virgin prairie 100 miles away in western Deaf Smith County near the New Mexico and Texas border.

Papa broke the land out, plowed under the indigenous grasses, and made a good crop. After years of difficult dryland farming, my parents' dream of owning their land and supporting a growing family was in sight.

Papa was a progressive farmer and bought a combine, a tractor, and a new farm truck two years later based on the promise of yet another bumper crop. We drove to church in our new truck on a sunny Sunday, October 20, 1929. All five older kids excitedly climbed up on the bed behind the truck's cab. Mama sat with Elton in the cab. My oldest brother Wilson stayed home.

After church, my 13-year-old sister Myrtice asked Papa if she could drive, and he agreed. Mama, six months pregnant, and the toddler, Elton, climbed in the cab with Myrtice.

Papa sat on a chair with us in the truck bed and held me on his lap. Eleven miles out of town, the steering rod broke, and the truck began weaving across the road. Papa leaned around and shouted to Myrtice, "What's wrong?" But it was too late. The truck careened into the ditch and crashed along this lonely road, miles from home and help.

This first hard lesson came when I was barely five and involved my whole family. The wreck injured everyone, and the most severely hurt were Papa and me. The lopsided truck threw us under the edge of the truck bed, pinning us to the ground.

Myrtice climbed out through the window of the driver's door. She assessed the damage and tried with all her might, but she could not lift the truck bed enough to free Papa or me. The little boys were crying, Mama was bleeding, so Myrtice took off running. She ran almost three miles before she found help.

Meanwhile, Papa talked to Mama, still under the wheel well on his stomach. They were true lovers, best friends, and co-owners of their farm. This impossible moment began their last goodbye. With his cheek pressed into the dusty road, he told her honestly, "I'm finished. I won't last."

While he gasped for breath, he gave her guidance: "Keep our children on the farm, bury me in Friona." He gave his young sons more instructions, "Mind your mama."

When help came, the farmers pulled Papa and me out from under the truck, further injuring his spinal cord and my hips. They laid us beside each other on a mattress. An ambulance arrived after a long wait and rushed us both to the hospital in Hereford.

Papa died later that day, and I suffered severe injuries. Mama had a broken wrist and deep facial lacerations, but mercifully, the baby she was carrying was safe.

Mama sat in quiet grief at the hospital, surrounded by women friends, who hoped she would fall asleep. She was now a widow, with six children from age 2 to 15, and was pregnant. She didn't sleep all night.

Her letters to Papa's family described how hard it was to arrive back at home where he had hammered every nail, built the house and sheds, and dug the holes for every fence post.

Mama reflected, "It seemed like the sun quit shining that day." Yet she built her life on a deep trust in God, which kept her disposition genuinely sunny.

A neighbor asked her what she did when she felt like breaking down.

"I couldn't do that in front of the children," she responded. Unbelievably, she controlled her expressions of grief for our security and happiness. She had little time or privacy to grieve.

Our farm was primitive and heavily in debt, yet Mama knew she had resources. Her primary resource was her faith that God, who is always good and loving, would provide. The crop coming in made payments on our loans for the new farm equipment. We fixed the vehicle involved in the wreck and used it within a week, providing necessary farming and transportation for years to come. She was always practical and never superstitious.

We owned chickens, a few workhorses, milk cows, and pigs. Mama gardened a large plot and fenced it in to protect her growing plants from the farm animals.

In our crowded home, filled now with Mama's brother Jimmy and his family who came to help, I miraculously recovered from my broken pelvis. Recovery was a long and painful process.

I cried in pain when anyone moved on the bed near me, so Mama slept on the quilt box in the living room, while Uncle Jimmy and Aunt Una slept on the other bed in my room. I remember intense pain when I moved or when others cared for me.

The doctor came and used two-by-fours to make a frame over my bed. A cloth swing hung from the structure and kept my hips steady about an inch above the mattress. He rigged pullies to keep weight on my broken hip and leg. A simple bucket of dirt hung at the end of my bed, providing the needed weight. No shiny medical apparatus for me!

Betty, my cousin, and my baby brother Elton were two years old and loved playing in the bucket of dirt. Their little hands digging in and moving the bucket made my broken bones hurt even more.

Mama expected things to go well for me. She believed by faith that I would get up and walk.

The doctor told Mama I might never walk again, but she never told me. She trusted God for healing mercies.

I remember her trying to sweep my bedroom as I lay on the bed recovering from my injuries. She was also injured and used one hand, holding the broom between her forearms to protect her healing wrist.

I got better within a month and limped painfully around the bed at first. Once I could move about, I slowly took a few steps and ventured out, holding onto furniture.

Mama expressed no pity for herself or me in our situation. She got up from the emotional tragedy of her loss and kept moving forward. And so did I.

My Application

Mama believed we would all recover and keep our land, even through the Great Depression, which was the second disaster in my life. Her faith deepened and grew, giving her a focus that kept us all moving in the right direction.

We were already garden farming, so we produced much of what we needed. Mama trusted the finances would work out, even when she had to put on her best dress, hat, and gloves and drive to town. At the bank, she negotiated extensions of our loans.

The depression lowered the price of our cream, eggs, and grain crops. As a result, we had to watch every penny. She kept every expenditure in a ledger.

Through it all, we observed Mama's character. She always kept her word. We knew she trusted God. She read to us from the Bible every evening, laughed with us, and sang around the bachelor stove that warmed our front room.

Despite being emotionally and physically injured, Mama worked right on through, keeping the garden and advising my older brother Wilson about the crops in the field.

I endured this second tragedy, the Great Depression, with everyone else in the whole world. It did not affect us as much because we had little money in the bank and none in the Stock Market.

The third tragedy that followed was devastating: the Dust Bowl. The wind blew unmercifully, and our little house was just a sifter, filling up with dirt. Sometimes, after a storm, we swept four or five five-gallon milk cans of sand and dust from each room. These dust storms occurred repeatedly through the 1930s.

We rejoiced when the rains came, thinking it was the end of our drought. But angry black clouds full of dirt returned time after time, killing our hopes and ruining our land. Again and again, the dark clouds rolled in, filling our house and burying roads and fences.

Mama soaked sheets in water and hung them over our beds—all without a complaint! She never made us feel we were a burden to her or that life was too hard. She even joined us outside in our games, playing in the sunset when the chores inside were finished.

Children quickly pick up on a disconnect between what adults say and what they do. She could not preach trust and be a worrier at the same time.

My hip healing was a miracle confirmed over 50 years later. When I had hip replacement surgery in the mid-1990s, the doctor told my husband, "I cannot understand how your wife ever walked on that hip. She endured a broken hip bone, and the ball of the femur shattered into the pelvic area."

His assessment of my injury, suffered decades before, was a sure witness to the power of Mama's faith and God's enabling me to walk. While bearing enormous sorrow, she trusted that God would give us hope and a future.

All of us children left home successfully, married, and had our own families. Like Mama, we lived out our dreams even through trials and troubles.

Scriptures to Consider

(All of the **Scriptures to Consider** will be taken from the Book of James, Nova's favorite book of the Bible since she was a young girl. At ninety-nine, she still requests evening scripture readings from the Book of James.)

Consider it pure joy, my brothers, whenever you face trials of many kinds, because you know the testing of your faith develops perseverance. Perseverance must finish its work so that you may be mature and complete, not lacking anything. Blessed is the man who perseveres under trial, because when he has stood the test, he will receive the crown of life that God has promised to those who love him. James 1:2-4, 12

1. When have you been able to see the testing of your faith as "pure joy"?

2. Is it easier to look back **later** at your former trials to consider them a joy? Why does the long-look perspective help us?

The Lord is a Faithful God

*So, the Lord must wait for you to come to Him,
so He can show you His love and compassion.
For the Lord is a faithful God.* **Isaiah 30:18**

Her children's path would never approach
  The vision they hoped for,
  But a recovery far beyond
  What they imagined.

Faith comes by living in the vision
  Of the love that is given,
  Living in hope
  Though it's torn in the living
  Building on the love
  Of a father long lost.

It would not be my choice,
  But You, loving Father
  Knew the brokenness
  Sown by his leaving,
  Would be less than the brokenness
  If he remained.

Faith that Your compassion
  Allowed the disaster,
  The ultimate breaking of many hearts
  Who found Your path forward.

As Your ways are
  Higher than our ways,
  So trust sows deeper
  Than the furrows he once plowed.

Your thoughts, precious to us,
  Are not our thoughts.
  You wait on us to come,
    So You can show us Your love and compassion.

Mevanee Parmer   *March 2024*

Family Memories and Redemption *from Mevanee*

When I published the family memoir of Grandmother Wyly's life in *Keep on the Sunny Side* in December 2019, I learned so much about my grandparents that I had never known. Yet I had been listening to the bare-bones version of their lives for years. I thought I knew everything about them.

The night before the tragic wreck, my grandfather Jim brought home a phonograph, which must have seemed magical to his six children—music dancing across the prairie! I had never heard that story, and Grandma had never shared it!

I knew Alta personally and spent years asking to hear stories of her life. She shared one or two minutes, only summaries. Yet I never knew what a peak in their lives my grandparents had reached when the tragedy happened.

In 1917, they had "starved out" in Gaines County, where they attempted to farm. Daddy Wilson came from Lockney and pleaded with them to move back and farm with him. This is yet another survival story I had never heard.

The future looked so bright in 1927 in Deaf Smith County. She and Jim had never seen such abundant wheat crops. How crushing the wreck must have been for her!

I underestimated her epic story of survival. It deepened my faith in God, who raised her up from the moment of seeming disaster to lead her family. And her path grew steeper through the Dust Bowl. She never told me about the historic wheat crops they enjoyed from 1927 to 1929.

Grandma was a sweet, meek person. But she possessed a surprising core of steel, a strength not apparent to me as her granddaughter. While watching Ken Burns' documentary *Dust Bowl*, Nova exclaimed, "What Mama did was miraculous!"

The series recounted many stories of Panhandle settlers full of despair, hopelessness, and anger. This bitterness was different from the attitude I heard from Grandma Wyly.

Nova's statement made me reassess everything I thought I knew about my grandmother. I knew we must save her faith, perseverance, and redemption story.

Jim and Alta's story, and Nova's, as well, move through the history of the Texas Panhandle, yet some of her great-grandchildren did not know the story. Now they can know. It is too rich a legacy to lose.

So, I admonish you, reader: write your family's stories! Start with even one short story, the briefest of memories, the stories told around the kitchen table, the stories you tell when everyone is together, the stories that make everyone blush or laugh or cry. Add all the details you can: the smells in the kitchen, the weather that day, the colors in the room, and the songs of the period.

Gathering your family stories unveils the realities they lived through, the jokes they told, the strengths they possessed, the rhythms of their lives, and the hymns they loved. Hidden behind their summaries are so many secrets that will surprise you.

I have helped edit several memoirs of Christian women who reveal that despite mistakes and insurmountable obstacles, the Lord, who is always good and faithful, redeems their lives' trials. Such redemption is not always conspicuous, but close examination and reflection disclose the truth of scripture: "We know that all things work together for the good of those who love God: those who are called according to His purpose." Romans 8:28 HCSB

When I Weary

When I weary of giving you care,
   I remember your clouded blue eyes
Lay once, sharply stinging with tears,
   As the truck bed pinned you to the road.

Five-year-old eyes,
   seeing too much pain and worry-
For over an hour, across a lifetime,
   waiting and hoping for help.

Those same blue eyes
   watched your parents' goodbyes,
Papa's cheek against the hard dust,
   unable to help you in your pain.

Did you hear his last words,
   "I won't make it"?
He who had hung your first swing
   was never again to lift you high.

We review those moments, you and I.
   You remind me that even with his back broken,
your Papa lifted his head
   to look at you—a last salute
to his daughter's blue eyes.

Those same eyes no longer see clearly,
   so you need care.
Yet soon you will see
   splendid sights--
Two fathers waiting:
   the face of the Papa
You last saw almost 100 years ago.

Your blue eyes, marvel
   before the Father who knit you together,
Hand in hand (can you imagine!)
   with Papa who died on the road.

So even when I'm weary, dear Father,
   my prayer is simple.
Help her see love from me.
   May her heart again rise,
this one who waited in anguish,
   Blue eyes looking down a long dirt road.

                    For my 99-year-old mother, Nova Vaughn
                    Mevanee Parmer   *February 2024*

This 1927 photograph captures Elton, my younger brother, and me. I entwine my hand casually around Elton's arm. Mama repeated as the photographer worked with us, "Hold on to the baby, Nova! Keep him from falling." I thought I was doing an excellent job and could not understand why Mama was so insistent. One little lurch and he would have landed on the floor. Mama entrusted us with responsibilities early in life. Two years after this sitting, the tragic wreck killed Papa and severely injured me.

Even in a remote corner of the Texas Panhandle, a rich community of relatives and friends blessed my family. I lived only a mile across the pasture from my Aunt Minnie and Uncle Everett. Their youngest daughter, Glenna, pictured here on the right, was my best friend. We remained close throughout our lives. She was outgoing and vivacious, while I was quiet and painfully shy as a teenager. We posed against the box-and-strip house Papa built. Glenna's face exudes confidence, while I look troubled and embarrassed at having to pose for the camera.

Lesson 2

Practice being unafraid,

and trust others

to step up to their responsibilities.

If Mama had been a fearful woman, we would not have lasted very long out on the prairie. The wind and coyotes howled through the night, rattlesnakes appeared under the chicken coop, and sorrows attacked her spirit. But she did not give up. This woman living alone with seven children walked bravely before us. She chose intentional courage.

How different the outcome would have been if she had succumbed to her loss and grief! The wreck left us all traumatized and injured, but Mama was determined to continue to give us each a good childhood and a good life.

One of my nieces asked Mama why she never remarried. Even when the opportunity for a new relationship came knocking, Mama refused. A man waited an appropriate length of time after Papa died. He carried flowers with him to visit. Mama sent him and his flowers packing.

She told my questioning niece, "Well, Honey, only a crazy man would marry a woman with seven children, and I didn't need a crazy man." She trusted God to meet her needs.

> ## Nova's Thoughts on Marriage
> (particularly to her unmarried grandchildren and great-grandchildren)
>
> If you marry for money, you'll earn every penny.
>
> It takes a mighty good man to beat no man at all.

Although she may not have known it, two of my older brothers, Bob and Porter, made a pact that if Mama remarried, they would leave and disappear down the road. She may have sensed that her five sons would struggle more if another man were around to give orders.

Mama wasn't afraid of doing without. She reminded me of the peasants in Tolstoy's novels.

Over one hundred years ago, he wrote about the life of the farmers of Russia. His book *Confession* noted, "I saw the whole life of these people passed in heavy labor, and that they were content with life — and they all knew the meaning of life and death, labored quietly, endured deprivations and sufferings and lived and died seeing therein not vanity, but good." (p. 57)

In *Renovation of the Heart*, Dallas Willard expanded on Tolstoy's comment. "The peasants whom Tolstoy admired so much were not yet swallowed up in modernity. They had solid traditions of faith and community that provided a ritual form of life and death. The result was that they knew what was good to do without regard to their feelings. Good was not determined for them by how they 'felt' or by what they thought was 'the best deal.' The overall order in which they lived usually gave them great strength and inner freedom derived from their sense of place and direction, even in the midst of substantial suffering and frustration." (p. 127)

Mama saw what needed to be done and joyfully did it. Caring for seven children required a vast amount of work. She met our physical and emotional needs and cared for the animals, the garden, and the fields with our help!

My grandmother Lula had prepared Mama to face her fears and knock them in the head. Mama had a fantastic memory and related the following story:

> When I was two, a mean old rooster harassed me. I was only a tiny girl. My mother told me, "Take this big stick and just hit that rooster as hard as you can. Kill him if you can."
>
> I went after the rooster, swinging as hard as I could. He left me alone after that. It was an important lesson in handling difficulties with action instead of letting a rooster pester me out of the chicken yard.

I saw Mama face life's problems, like that attacking rooster. And she stood up to them with a big stick. Truth be told, sometimes that big stick was full of grace!

One night, she heard our dog Sparky barking down near the barn. She told Wilson and Porter, her oldest boys, "Go out there and see what's happening. Sparky is barking like it's a stranger." They went out and found our neighbor, Hal, in the barn.

Hal asked Wilson, "What are you boys doing here?"

Wilson replied, "No, Hal. The question is, what are you doing here?" He stole cow cake (feed compressed into small cakes) from a widow with seven children!

After that, Hal still came around our place. If he happened to appear near mealtime, Mama invited him to join all eight of us at the table. She put a ninth plate on the table if he stayed, so he ate with us! She hit that problem in the head with compassion. We learned forgiveness, generosity, and hospitality from her example of serving our errant neighbor and his family.

She did not think of us as needy. We had plenty of fields and, therefore, plenty of food. We had cows, chickens, and pigs. Instead of fearfully hoarding, Mama used her resources to meet our needs and cheerfully give to others.

Her hospitality extended to our school friends, who loved to come home with us. She encouraged and enjoyed our wild and raucous play and sometimes joined in. Our water fight got the bedding wet but did not dampen her spirits. She helped us hang out the wet sheets and blankets and knew the wind and sun would dry them quickly.

Mama was not afraid of unexpected accidents. Once, when we played jacks at the table at night, one of us swung wide for the ball. A little hand caught the lamp globe, knocked it over, and shattered it.

Mama stopped writing her letter at the other end of the table, helped us clean up the glass, and continued writing by the flickering flame of the globe-less lamp. I am still amazed that her children's mistakes did not fluster her.

She never yelled at us. She accepted our many childish mishaps and knew they were bound to happen. They were part of growing up.

Mama was not afraid of her mistakes, even when they caused her pain. Once, Mama's tomato catsup was bubbling away in the pressure cooker. She hadn't firmly screwed the lid down.

As she wrestled with the top to reset it, the whole pot of catsup exploded in her face. She had terrible burns but didn't panic. I boiled tea leaves quickly, cooled them, and gently applied them all over her face. Amazingly, she was uncomplaining throughout the whole procedure.

Still in pain, she told us, with her matter-of-fact attitude, that we'd better head for the doctor. He treated her, told me

I'd done an excellent job with the tea leaves, and put her under a light tent.

She recuperated at her sister's house, and I had to cook for my five brothers. She knew there would be too much pressure if she came home just looking around at all she needed to do.

I went to see her shortly after the accident. I cried when I couldn't recognize her swollen face, covered with red blisters. She didn't use this as an excuse when she got home. She still cooked, canned, dried, and preserved foods. But she was more careful. Her face healed with barely a scar.

Mama was not fearful of unsettling setbacks. She didn't let them disturb her sense of peace. Right after the howling winds of the Dust Bowl pounded the Panhandle, our well went dry. The family's workload was even more difficult. The boys hauled water from Uncle Everett's well about a mile away for several years.

During all that time, Mama didn't panic or wring her hands. She moved her garden to Uncle Everett and Aunt Minnie's, where water was readily available. Listening for the wind to come up at night, she lit a lantern and walked by moonlight over to the garden.

There, she turned on the water at their windmill to keep her produce growing and walked back home to sleep, knowing she had done all she could to keep her family fed.

Finally, Wilson ran into Mr. Adams in town, where they ran errands. Mr. Adams asked Wilson how things were going, and Wilson explained that our well had dried up.

Mr. Adams responded, "If you ever got water from that well, I can probably fix it. And if I can't, there'll be no charge."

Wilson explained that we didn't have a way to pay him, and Mr. Adams said he'd take an extra pig or some chickens in payment. He came by shortly after that and fixed the well.

After Papa's death, my oldest brother, Wilson, stepped up and managed the farm. Mama entrusted him with enormous responsibilities. She had to. His work saved our farm and supported our family. A book about the boy who grew up overnight and led his family through the Dust Bowl should be written.

Mama knew her voice could calm our fears. Once, after an extended trip to stay with relatives in Santa Fe, I was happy to be back home. But after Mama and I had gone to bed, I heard the wind howling across the roof of our home, something I hadn't heard in Santa Fe. I expressed to Mama, "I'm afraid of the wind!"

"You don't need to be afraid! Our roof creaks a lot. It's okay." Since she always spoke the truth, I was no longer upset about the wind and went to sleep.

I rested blissfully that night, listening to the grinding of the windmill, the chirping of the cricket behind the water shelf, and the flicker of the cottonwood tree. It was music to my ears.

Mama was a writer and list keeper. She kept a steady stream of letters flowing to her siblings and old friends in Lockney. This network of friends was one of her emotional supports. She always shared these letters with us, so we felt part of an extended network of loving people.

The church people were essential to us. Their fellowship, friendship, and generosity sustained us. They were not wealthy but shared as much as they could, especially their love and encouragement.

Mama's sister, Minnie, and brother-in-law, Everett Jack, were great encouragers. Uncle Everett could be quite a rascal. Once, when I had joined their family for supper, I wanted Glenna to come over to spend the night. He said, "She can come if you'll give me a kiss."

I thought about this for a while, yet I dreaded kissing Uncle. But I wanted Glenna to come over.

Finally, I got up and walked over to kiss his cheek as he sat finishing supper. But he kept ducking away from me and making my task impossible.

He grimaced like my kiss would kill him, which made everyone laugh except me. He finally let me plant a tiny, quick peck on his cheek, and Glenna came home with me overnight.

My Application

My most spiritually significant step during my early years involved an icy horse tank. In January 1939, after I turned 14, I was baptized by one of the visiting ministers, J. T. Corder.

I had considered my commitment for over a year. I was painfully shy and didn't want to cry in front of church friends. I also hated being the center of any event. But my convictions overcame these feelings.

Eva Chiles insisted that I put on her heavy cotton coat as we walked to the tank. I started to take it off before I stepped into the water, but she said I should wear it. The water was so cold that my brothers broke ice off the top and lifted clear, thin slices to the ground.

My commitment that day was an essential part of my walk with Jesus, which would be tested when I became an adult. I remember immediately afterward. I started reading the book of James. The book was full of practical applications.

The Bible teaches Jesus' followers to live without fear. Mama lived without fear, so I also learned to be fearless. I graduated from Friona High School at 16.

I knew of no other girls who attended college from our area except my cousin Glenna and my sister Myrtice. Many parents felt it wasn't a wise investment for their daughters, who would marry quickly and become homemakers. Mama deemed it essential for my older sister, Myrtice, and me to attend college. After all, she was suddenly thrust into the breadwinning role without warning.

Myrtice attended Amarillo College and West Texas State University in Canyon, Texas. Once, Mama and I did errands in Amarillo and stopped by Myrtice's room in Canyon. Mama gave Myrtice her last dime. Mama taught me to support others, even if it's your last dime.

Being dauntless served me well when I went to Texas Technological College in Lubbock at 16. I never even thought to be afraid. I paid $8 a month for a shared bedroom with kitchen privileges. As we say in the Panhandle, I was "living in high cotton." We had a telephone, indoor plumbing, a bathtub with hot and cold running water, electric lights, and a radio without the bother of batteries, which were always running down. I had grown up without any of these amenities.

I immediately began attending church. I watched Mama lean into friendships through the years, so it was also natural for me.

Some friends recommended Redell Parks as an ideal roommate for me. She showed me where my classes were and introduced me to new friends. In my second year at Tech, I lived in a co-op house, Casa Linda. The girls administered the house and did all the cleaning and cooking.

Mama's fearless example endured with me through the years. Many decades later, living alone in Amarillo, my neighborhood was the scene of some gruesome murders. The killer targeted women living alone, like me. My daughter called from Illinois and begged, "Mom, be careful. Lock your doors and windows. And please give up your evening walks!"

"No," I insisted. I will not let some criminal make me a prisoner in my own home." Although I was cautious and locked my doors and windows, I walked before sunset and felt safe. I felt sure of God's protection and care.

Mama taught us God wants us to trust Him for our needs. He assures us He will keep us safe, even though we walk through the valley of the shadow of death. Fear has its place in our emotions. It warns us of impending danger! But a fearful mindset is a heavy burden we must not carry.

Scriptures to Consider

Believers in humble circumstances ought to take pride in their high position. But the rich should take pride in their humiliation—since they will pass away like a wild flower. For the sun rises with scorching heat and withers the plant; its blossom falls, and its beauty is destroyed. In the same way, the rich will fade away even while they go about their business. Blessed is the one who perseveres under trial, because, having stood the test, that person will receive the crown of life that the Lord has promised to those who love him. James 1:9-12

1. How might these words have comforted Mama? How does God view the poor of this world?

Speak and act as those who are going to be judged by the law that gives freedom, because judgment without mercy will be shown to anyone who has not been merciful. Mercy triumphs over judgment. James 2:12-13

2. How was Mama rich in faith and mercy? How did her mercy triumph over judgment?

Life's Ironies *from Mevanee*

Grandma Wyly's self-reliance, independence, and determination are oft-lauded virtues that helped her survive the Dirty Thirties. Yet these qualities also increased her suffering. Had she allowed Mr. Guinn, a county commissioner, to give her help when he offered, life might have been easier for her children.

When Mr. Guinn came by, she told him to "help those who need it. We have food in our bellies and clothes on our backs. Not everyone in this county does."

She walked over to her purse, took out a few coins, and offered them to Mr. Guinn for the poor, which she and her children decidedly were not! She was determined that her family would never be caught living on charity.

She was also approached twice by an attorney, once right after the wreck and again just before her youngest child, Duane, turned 18. They encouraged her to sue the Chevrolet Company, which produced the truck and the faulty steering drive system. Undoubtedly the break in the steering rod caused the tragic accident.

Such a settlement might have allowed her to move her children into a larger, warmer house. From 1927 to 1945, she lived in the small "chicken house" Papa had built as a temporary shelter when he first moved to the acreage.

She refused to sue for her benefit. America was not as litigious then as it is now. Myrtice quipped once, "We were poor, but so were all our neighbors."

Those qualities helped Grandma Wyly persevere into old age, paying her own way to the end. Yet her independence greatly increased the difficulties she and her children faced during the Dust Bowl years.

Overcoming difficulties ultimately led to their strength of character — and Grandma Wyly was all about character!

Sixteen-year-old me in college! I left the farm for Texas Tech, elated to have the opportunity of college and new friendships. I went from living in a home with no running water, toilet, and electricity to having all those amenities and a telephone line! I had a new church family, including many students from Tech. I was living in "high cotton."

I'm the second on the left, and the housemate sitting at my end of the couch had just said something to make us all laugh. These were my Casa Linda sisters. We lived in a big communal house and shared chores. Many were majors in home economics, but the English majors always cooked the most delicious meals.

I just said, "I do." And I was so happy. Odell Purdy and I were married on August 12, 1944, at Uncle Everett and Aunt Minnie Jack's home. We shared a double wedding with their daughter, Glenna, and her fiancé, Arlon Miller. Odell and I honeymooned in New Mexico and immediately moved to our new teaching jobs in Clauene, Texas.

Lesson 3

Children are not pets,

but real people

who are going to have to make

their own way in the real world.

Does pet care prepare us for parenting? I have heard people say that! Dogs and cats will tolerate a lack of attention. And pets stay cute and cuddly most of their lives.

Babies come home from the hospital all cute and cuddly. But after thirty minutes, new parents must feed, burp, diaper, and rock the baby. The new little one is sleepy and sweet, but only when fed, warm, and dry, which requires hard labor, sleep deprivation, and continuous attention.

Parents play a crucial role in the growth and development of their children, from infancy to the challenging teenage years.

Parents usually enjoy cute and cuddly little ones, but an inattentive parent pays a high price as children grow older. Bonding with a 10- or 15-year-old demands solid devotion, prayer, and energy. Every child, from infancy through the difficult teenage years, needs a responsive, thoughtful, and prayerful adult.

When Papa died in 1929, Mama became that steady adult for all seven children. At the time of the wreck, she was pregnant with my youngest brother, Duane, and had to assume the many farm management responsibilities—with my 15-year-old brother Wilson.

She had children of all stages and ages in her home. Her unwavering love was a sure foundation and a steadying force in our lives.

We children saw the daily discipline of heart and character in Mama. Please note that the word teenager was not commonly used when I was a teenager. Mama didn't say, "Oh, they're just teenagers! What can you expect?" She expected a lot. She didn't consider any age an excuse for bad behavior.

Children move from childhood to young adulthood without getting labeled as teenagers. Of course, I had my share of timidity, moods, and fears. A word of explanation or encouragement from Mama could quell my insecurities.

Given the heavy workload on the farm, we had to take on responsibilities, which was beneficial. We all felt needed in the family.

The day began with Mama calling the boys to dress in work clothes and head to the barn to milk the cows. As young as seven or eight years old, the boys helped with milking, then came in and poured the milk through the creamer, put on school clothes, had breakfast, and headed to the bus.

The Dust Bowl hit in 1931. When dust storms covered Mama's garden plants, she got out, shook the dirt off them, and propped them up. Yet Mama seldom complained or moaned to us. She knew we did not need the added stress.

If I saw my mother's sadness, I immediately asked, "What's wrong, Mama?" The anxious look vanished from her face, and she immediately reassured me with a smile or a song. One of her favorite songs was "Keep on the Sunny Side." It included a verse that mirrored our situation:

> Though the storm and its fury broke today,
> Crushing hopes that we cherished so dear,
> Storm and cloud will, in time, pass away,
> The sun again will shine bright and clear.

She acknowledged the storms but assured us that we lived in a land where "the sun again will shine bright and clear."
Although she raised seven children with great love, she knew we could not be pampered. Life's realities would hit one day, and she modeled courage during danger and hard times. She kept walking with the Lord. We saw that He was her strength. Philippians 2:14 says, "Do everything without complaining or arguing." She did not allow herself or us to complain or grumble.
Once, when she had only oatmeal on hand for supper, the boys came home from the fields in the evening. One of the boys said derisively, "Is this all we're having for supper?"
Mama would not let that slip by. "Son, this is not what you're having for supper. You are going to bed without supper." And that is what happened! We enjoyed the oatmeal with hand-churned butter, fresh cream, and sugar.
Even with chores and responsibilities piled heavily on her shoulders, Mama listened to us. She was interested in what we were doing and paid attention to what was happening in our hearts.

My Application

By the time I had children, things had changed in America. Economically, we were much wealthier. The days of the Great Depression and the Dust Bowl had ended, and we who lived through them were grateful to see them over.

At Texas Tech, I met Odell Purdy on my first day of registration. Redell introduced us, and we dated for almost three years.

Once, we stayed out too late and missed curfew. My penalty was to wash all the walls and baseboards in every room of my rooming house, Casa Linda. Odell came over and helped me with the rooms where young men were allowed, which made the tedious chore full of laughter.

He took me home by train to Quitaque to meet his parents on their farm in Hall County. He carried water from the well to the stove for his mother. She had no running water in her kitchen. Odell told me his dad liked me because I was a quiet girl.

In August of 1944, we married and left Lubbock behind. Odell graduated with a bachelor's degree in science. Although I accumulated over 100 hours of classes, I did not finish my degree. I received a teaching certification, which allowed me to work in public schools.

Immediately after our honeymoon in August, we moved to Clauene, Texas, a rural community a few miles south of Levelland. I taught grades three and four. Odell taught high school classes, drove the bus, worked as a custodian when needed, and met with county authorities as the principal. He preached in various congregations on weekends and hoped to find a permanent minister's position.

Lampasas Church of Christ hired Odell in 1945, so we moved there when school wrapped up in Clauene. In Kempner, a short drive from Lampasas, I taught first through fourth grades with 15 students. I enjoyed the sweet country kids. The students were easy to direct, and we all had fun.

The following year, I taught in Lampasas and had 48 second graders. Laws limiting the size of classes came later. Many could not speak English but spoke only Spanish. It was a most challenging year.

I asked my principal what to do with so many children, some far above the average age of second graders. She told me to use the paddle, which I did reluctantly. I wish I had told them more stories and sung songs with them.

We moved to Seagraves, Texas, near the New Mexico border in 1948. I taught second grade again and loved my students. The church family there was sweet and loving. Our first son, Ira, was born while we lived there, and our daughter Mevanee was born 13 months later. I didn't plan that too well. I washed diapers for two babies by hand!

From the early days of our marriage, we agreed to live on only one of our salaries. I always planned to stay home with our children and provide a house full of peace and love, just as my mother had. I taught school for four years before we started our family.

In 1950, we moved to Turkey, Texas, to a small farming community in Hall County. Odell's parents farmed nearby, and the children loved spending time at their farm south of town. Odell became sought out as a dynamic gospel preacher and held meetings all over the Texas Panhandle and western Oklahoma. Our son Alan Wynn was born in 1954 while we lived in Turkey.

In late 1954, we were asked to move to Forest Hill Church of Christ in Amarillo, Texas. This small church on the north side of Amarillo served the community along Highway 66. We had several families from the SAC wing of the air base in northeast Amarillo.

We bought a new home across from Whittier Elementary, where all three children attended. We made trips to California and Oregon, holding meetings for several congregations on each trip.

I was a stay-at-home mom for 23 years. We had three children in five years, and I took my job seriously. I realized I had only one crack at mothering three kids.

We worked hard to instill integrity and determination in our children. We wanted them to solve problems and love God, His Word, and His church. We tried to be diligent and consistent, knowing that an inconsistent example doesn't work.

The children sat in church with us from infancy and knew almost all the songs in the songbook.

One memorable bedtime incident revealed their love for hymns, but misunderstanding of some of them. My three-year-old daughter insisted, "Mama, sing us the 'Ready at Thy Bedtime' song. You know, that song we sing at church."

I asked my four-year-old son to translate. As the oldest, he often had to interrupt her words, which were a mystery to us.

"She means that 'Here a mouse and me' song." Ira tried explaining her words to me, but he didn't know the words either.

I finally realized she was trying to say, "Ready at Thy bidding." He meant, "Here am I, send me," the words to the old hymn, "Lord, Send Me." I tried to explain the words and their meanings, but they were still unsure. We all laughed and sang through the song again.

We taught the children that life is fun and that we find true family in church, regardless of race or income. Once, during a span of two weeks, we went to church forty times. My youngest son, Alan, told me, "Mama, I'm all churched out!"

Odell held a youth meeting in the mornings, followed by games and lunch, and another lesson in the afternoon. The evening closed out with a gospel meeting, which included singing hymns, praying, and a rousing sermon.

We were careful not to air the church's troubles in front of our children. If I criticized someone, that person might be vital to them in their walk of faith. Any negative comments I made of others could come full circle and hurt my children.

Our children had no idea of the daily hardships of my childhood. I told them the stories, but they were too young to imagine my life in the 1930s. Society now suggests that we must make life as comfortable as possible for our children.

I believe children need to persevere through difficulties and endure. I trained my children to deal with rudeness and have a witty verbal come-back. Mama taught me to say something back to bullies at school even if my words didn't make sense! She'd say, "Don't let them think they got your goat!" I learned to use her advice often, especially with my five pesky brothers.

I expected my children to live differently because of their faith. They should act thoughtfully toward others, showing love and respect.

When a kid repeatedly attacked my son Ira during physical education class at school, we prayed and told him to respond boldly. We suggested he land a punch if needed and confront his bully. And be sure to do it right in front of the coach, not in some dark corner of the gym.

Before Ira left that morning, we prayed about the problem. When he came home that afternoon, he walked about a foot off the ground. The bully seemed to sense my son's new resolve and hadn't bothered him that day.

In the fourth grade, my daughter, Mevanee, complained about a demanding elementary school teacher and begged to be removed from that class. I left her with the teacher.

She didn't like it, but I wanted her to see she could work through difficulties and what she perceived as unfairness. She did well in the class and learned to enjoy the projects that demanded thinking outside the box.

The behavior of my youngest son, Alan, gave us deep concern. As a toddler, he perfected the behavior of passing out. If someone didn't hand over the toy he wanted, he held his breath, turned blue, and fell over, remaining unconscious for several seconds.

We were so concerned that we consulted a doctor, who told us to keep him happy, preventing the episodes. Later, when we checked back in with the doctor, we mentioned that we had kept Alan from having these passing-out fits, except for a few times when he didn't get his way quickly enough.

"Oh," the pediatrician responded, "I see. Well, the next time he wakes up from passing out, make sure he's uncomfortable." We followed his directions, although it was hard. Those fainting fits ended almost immediately.

It matters how you raise your children, how they are disciplined, and whether they feel loved and listened to. Training is crucial at each developmental stage.

Simple, dependable routines helped us. Meals were a good time to teach our youngsters manners, conversation skills, and good nutrition. I started each day with a warm breakfast and a cheering word to give my kids a helpful start for their day's adventures. That is what my mother had provided, even during the most challenging times.

We kept a little box of "Daily Bread" Bible verses on the table. One of us pulled out a card and read the verse over breakfast. Alan said that meant a lot to him as he marched off to elementary school.

We always sat down together for supper, even if it was a simple meal of tomato soup and grilled cheese sandwiches. We shared our experiences and thoughts, providing necessary closure for each day.

You only get one chance at raising civilized human beings. Mama knew that children must be taught, coached, and loved. The opportunities are rich when children are young.

Babies and toddlers are not pets. They develop their habits, personalities, and character from birth and need attention, direction, and encouragement from the moment they arrive.

Parents fall in love with their children if they bond with them. Children are not random beings but precious people created by God. They are at their best when they find their identity in God's perspective of them.

All too fast, our children are grown and gone. I'm so grateful for the years I gave up my career and stayed home with my children. After my kids left home, I was blessed with plenty of years to enjoy and develop my teaching and social work careers.

Most women today don't get the luxury of staying home, but children are our most lasting and precious treasures.

Scriptures to Consider

Who is wise and understanding among you? Let him show it by his good life, by deeds done in the humility that comes from wisdom. But the wisdom that comes from heaven is first of all pure; then peace-loving, considerate, submissive, full of mercy and good fruit, impartial and sincere. Peacemakers who sow in peace raise a harvest of righteousness. James 3:13, 17-18

1. Why is humility essential in raising a family?

2. What kinds of good deeds can we do with our children? Why is teaching them all along the way important?

The Blessing of Having a Mom at Home *from Mevanee*

Although my parents faced challenges at work and home, we children were protected from any sense of insecurity by the surety that my mother was ever present, watchful, and relaxed. She lived in a simpler time when most women chose to stay home and didn't have to work outside the home. We regularly visited friends' homes, and I was often amazed at the different atmospheres in families—not bad necessarily, but very different.

Our parents took us camping and boating in nature, maybe not realizing how powerful those activities are to calm the soul. During the days on North Marrs in Amarillo, we could play outside all day and only come in for meals or a drink. What a sadly different world we live in now! Adults must be on guard, watching out for various dangers in schools, at home, and especially on their children's phones.

My mother was usually home when we came in from school. I remember the smell of apricot fried pies wafting through the house one brisk autumn afternoon. The apricots came from our backyard. The house was tidy, with the wash done and the kitchen clean.

I remember visiting two friends after school whose mothers worked full-time and arrived late in the afternoon, worn and frazzled. I didn't like the feeling of the stale, empty house and felt sorry for my friends.

They came home daily to breakfast dishes still in the sink, beds unmade, and the wash sorted in piles on the floor. Sometimes, their mothers arrived home already stressed and tired, with a day's worth of chores waiting. My friends whose mothers worked had a very different childhood than mine.

When I became a mother, I stayed home for most of my children's early years. I loved being home with them for relaxed mornings, not rushing them to daycare.

A generation later, when I began teaching school, I realized how much mothers had supported the educational process in the 1950s. We expected extravagant parties on all the major holidays, with several mothers arriving to serve refreshments and lead games. Our field trips had plenty of volunteer chaperones. Most mothers worked outside the home when I taught school in the 1990s. I noted a big difference in children's experiences.

I Always Wake Up in a Room with My Mother

Before birth, I know we are due.
One Umbilical cord unites our beating hearts.
Our brains share blood and oxygen,
 songs and rhythms, faith and refuge,
 perceptions of the world to a fledgling view.

My bed is warm, the room cozy,
 but hers was stacked with quilts,
 and still was so cold that snow made
horizontal lines across the covers. She is buried
in depths of fabric, hand-stitched by thread.
Her head hardly visible, is hidden by layers

I've been in her room since birth. She also lay
 from birth in a room with her mother,
 through her farming youth until a quiet leaving.
My mother's light scent now is almond lotion,
 and mild soap, her hair softly splayed.

She snores lightly, just like her mother.
The kindness of her days is our shared dream.
My daughters now seamlessly snuggle-swirl subconsciously.
Our world's curious delight is the way
 we each wake up in a room with one another.

Swaddled in years of traditions,
 stretching to the floor, hands to the Lord,
 mind firmly settled, braiding the hair,
 in habits of life, kept firm over time
 in the minds of a long line of women.

I always wake up in a room with my mother.
Mevanee Parmer   August 2024

After teaching school, Odell quickly found work in the ministry in Lampasas, Texas. I taught in Kempner, then in Lampasas. Later, we moved to Seagraves. I taught second grade again. We had lots of fun and entertained many guests on a newlywed budget. Below is my "school" picture from the 1947-1948 school year.

This photograph captures part of my family, the Wyly clan. We have made it through the Dust Bowl by the grace of God. Back Row: Left to right are Bob Wyly, Harris Evans, Iva Waters Wyly, and Wilson Wyly. In front are me, Myrtice Wyly Evans holding onto James, Wilson and Iva's son. Mama is next holding Wilson (W.H.) Evans, Myrtice's baby, and Porter Wyly.

Lesson 4

With a positive attitude and hard work,

you can do about anything

with almost nothing,

and have a good time doing it.

The wreck occurred on October 20, 1929, and was followed nine days later by the stock market crash. We hardly noticed the national panic, which did not affect us much since we owned no stock. However, it brought on the Great Depression, which reduced grain prices, as well as cream, eggs, and livestock prices.

Mama taught us how to make a life using every resource we had to the best advantage. She patterned this for us in the months following Papa's death, which was more challenging for her than the Depression and Dust Bowl. But she found ways to survive without him.

Writers often depict Depression-era people as dour and incapable of joy. But Mama knew we thrived on simple, home-spun pleasures. After supper, she sometimes came outside and played jump rope, hide-and-seek, and other games with us. In winter, she played indoors, dominoes, and our favorite, carrom. My brothers made a carrom board in their high-school shop class. The game is like mini billiards.

Mama made cheese, sauerkraut, hogshead cheese, and sausage—items we buy now at the grocery store. She raised a garden and canned various fruits and vegetables, but she had no water hose! She scraped dirt furrows with her hoe and directed the water from the windmill down to the garden.

Sometimes, when I arrived home hungry after school, the house was filled with the aroma of beans cooked with ham hocks. Mama often opened a half-gallon jar of her canned pickles to complete this welcome snack. Her spicy-sweet bread-and-butter pickles were my favorite.

She often stirred up a recipe for a thrifty one-egg cake. She also made her tomato sauce, catsup, jams, and jellies. She dried apples, even using the apple cores, to make jelly.

Mama made the most of everything. When she served up fried chicken, her boys said, "When Mama cleans a chicken, all that's left is the cackle."

Mama sewed continually at her little treadle machine. She made clothes and rag dolls for me and crocheted doilies. Her hands were busy, her focus on what she could accomplish.

Most importantly, she enjoyed her work and her chores. She hung a quilting frame, which could be lowered from the ceiling in the living room when she found time to quilt. She constructed her quilts from scraps that cost her "very little to nothing."

Imagine seven children, very few household conveniences, and time to quilt! She knew the importance of taking breaks and creating vacation days. One outing we all enjoyed was a campout at a cottonwood grove where trees grew in the breaks.

We traveled just an hour north of our place, made camp, kindled a fire, and slept under the stars. We owned no fancy camping gear but brought blankets, quilts, and a skillet from home. We sang songs together into the vast prairie sky. The star-gazing party was a wonderful respite from the monotony of chores.

Other times, Mama built a fire down by our draw and cooked outside, frying potatoes, onions, and a little ham. We thought that was a grand supper.

She knew the importance of friends and community. She practiced the old saying "You've got to be a friend to have a friend." Her church and Home Demonstration Club were a network that cost her nothing, yet they offered significant support for our entire family.

My Application

When I was first married, my husband and I worked as teachers in Clauene. I regularly offered hospitality and fed lots of visitors on a small budget.

After church on Sunday, we saved up a dime to buy special store-bought white bread if we had company over. In the 1940s, store-bought bread was considered a special treat.

Later, my husband became a full-time minister. We never made much money, but our thrifty upbringing was valuable.

We always lived on my husband's salary, even when I worked. When they were little, I knew I wanted to stay home with my children for as long as possible. If we entitled ourselves to a two-salary lifestyle, staying home with my kids would feel impossible.

People were generous to us. Farmer friends at Seagraves and Turkey gave us mountains of green beans, corn, and even quail, which we canned, froze, or cooked fresh to save on the grocery bill. I sewed my daughter's and my dresses regularly, saving quite a bit.

Even though I wasn't working, we saved up and bought two quarter-sections of land near Mama and Papa's original farm. Although it was not a huge investment, we rented our land to my family members and sometimes placed it in government programs. The land has always helped us with income.

As our children entered their preteens, we bought a motorboat for under $100. Once again, I found children thrive on simple pleasures. We taught them, our church members, and many relatives how to water ski on Buffalo Lake, an hour from our home in Amarillo.

We enjoyed many hours together on the water. We all loved being at the lake—camping, fishing, and boating. We camped regularly in a simple tent with family and friends.

Once, a couple of church members complained that we had the money for a boat, and they didn't. My husband flatly told them that if they stopped smoking and saved their cigarette money, they could buy a boat like ours in a year or less.

They were incredulous. Odell multiplied the numbers to show them how much their smoking habit cost them.

I used Mama's lessons of thrifty living throughout my life, especially in rearing my children. Fun is often free. Creating a warm, cheery home does not require a stash of cash. If Mama had complained and moaned about our circumstances, we would have had a different view of life.

Mama and I taught our children to live well in this land full of freedom and opportunity, even on a modest income. With a positive attitude and hard work, you can do just about anything with almost nothing and have a good time doing it.

Scriptures to Consider

Be patient, then, brothers, until the Lord's coming. See how the farmer waits for the land to yield its valuable crop and how patient he is for the autumn and spring rains. You, too, be patient and stand firm because the Lord's coming is near. Don't grumble against each other, brothers, or you will be judged. The Judge is standing at the door. James 5:7-9

1. How is our patience a testimony to our children?

2. What are some of the consequences when we are impatient?

Growing Up in the 1950s *from Mevanee*

Just as I could not imagine my mother's life, joys, and hardships on the farm, my children can hardly imagine my life as a child. I grew up in church, which was a very happy place. My parents were faithful, loving people, and I assumed most homes were as happy as ours.

Occasionally, we overheard counseling situations, which let me know people had struggles, but as a child, I felt free of those. Our heroes were the aging minister, Alva Johnson, and the young missionary families, B. and Ruth Shelburne and Roland and Wanda Hayes who went to Malawi, Africa to serve at Namikango Mission.

My parents were thrifty and wise, but besides wearing homemade dresses, I felt secure. The whole family rejoiced when we made the last payment on the farmland we purchased as an investment. We enjoyed water skiing several times a week at Buffalo Lake and loved the week-long tent camping trips to Lake Altus.

If I count both my mom's and dad's sides of the family, I have almost 50 cousins. I consider them all one of the great joys of my growing years. Most children today can hardly imagine all the fun cousins can be.

My best friend, Ginger, was a dear girl from church. We enjoyed overnights, bike rides, and long chats. I thought our families were very similarly happy. From her early teens, she understood some hard secrets that I did not, and she never shared them, at least not with me. I thought we both lived in ideal families that shared faith and fun.

Ironically, I never knew until I was married and over 22 years old that my mother struggled to hold things together in her marriage for years.

Grandmother Wyly protected her younger children from carrying the weight of her grief and the reality of finances. My mother protected us from the wounds she bore in those years while we were teenagers.

By 1979, I was on a new and unexpected path in life. God had made a way for me through the wilderness and the pain of divorce. He led me through green pastures and quiet waters of blessing.

Lesson 5

When you are down, get up and begin to put one foot in front of the other.

My life has been blessed by women who refused to focus on their circumstances. Mama did not let life's difficulties dictate her faith or her choices. Her mother, Lula Lile Wilson, and grandmother, Kate Mugg Lile were strong women who faced overwhelming challenges.

Their example led Mama to choose a hard path after Papa's death. She could have given up the farm and saved herself a mountain of hard labor. Sometime after the tragic wreck, her brother Lee offered us a place in his home near downtown Santa Fe, New Mexico.

He and his wife started a business there in the late 1920s, raised many children, and sheltered many others. They offered to take us in to live in a real house with conveniences nearby. Instead, Mama made up her mind to stay on the farm.

I am certain Mama made her decision based on two things: 1) Papa's instructions with his last breath to keep us all on the farm, and 2) what would be best for us children.

When the truck tragically flipped over, my oldest brother, Wilson, was 15; my oldest sister, Myrtice, who drove the truck that day, was 13. Porter was next at 10, Bob was 8, I was 5, and Elton was 2. Perhaps Mama could not imagine raising 7 children in a busy city.

In any case, Mama's reply to Uncle Lee's offer was, "I appreciate your generous offer. But I feel my children will be better off staying here on the farm. In Santa Fe, I wouldn't know where my boys were." The issue was simple: she wanted to know where her children were and what they were doing. At the farm, annual fieldwork, gardening, and livestock kept us all busy and within the sound of her voice.

The tiny house Papa built was supposed to be a temporary shelter. Although it was well-built for a tool and chicken shed, we awakened to little trails of snow crossing our bed covers, straight white lines that came through the box-and-strip construction.

In summer, we had no air conditioning and worked in the heat. The two bedrooms were tiny, and three or four people shared each room. The "chicken coop," as Papa called it, was primitive: no running water, toilet, or electricity.

During the Dust Bowl, after the storms came, we carried four or five 5-gallon buckets of sand from each room. Many neighbors fled this area to California or other states. Mama stayed on despite friends giving up their farms. She banked her future on the directions Papa gave her. In the face of disaster, she trusted the wisdom of his dying wish.

Duane was born February 1, 1930, three months after Papa's death. He was a welcome, cheerful baby.

Another example of Mama's faith is shown in her words to Duane during a hailstorm. Nine-year-old Duane and

Mama were at home alone one Sunday afternoon in June 1939. Suddenly, a storm blew up, and Duane recorded the effects of the storm on his heart and spiritual life:

> We had a good wheat crop for the first time in many years, and harvest was fast approaching.
>
> On Sunday afternoon, my older brothers, Wilson, Porter, and Bob had gone to move the combine to a field some four or five miles away to start harvesting within a day or two. Wilson was married and worked at his farm down the road, but he used our combine and helped Porter and Bob with the farming chores.
>
> While they were gone, a storm of rain and hail came up at the home. Within 20 minutes, the wheat that had been two-and-a-half feet high was hailed out. Only straw stubs were left standing.
>
> Mama and I stood in the old house's front door and watched the good crop's destruction. I was devastated and turned to Mama with tears, saying, "Mom, what are we going to do?"
>
> She put her arm around me and said, "Son, the Lord has always cared for us. We have always made it with His help, and we will continue to make it--without this crop." Her calm response had a profound impact on my life.

Dallas Willard's book, **_Renovation of the Heart,_** described people who lived like Mama. He stated,

> Try to remember the situations in which we find ourselves are never as important as our responses to them, which come from our "spiritual" side. A carefully cultivated heart

will, assisted by the grace of God, foresee, forestall, or transform most of the painful situations before which others stand like helpless children saying "Why?" p. 14.

Mama gave another example of a calm approach to life's problems: My brothers were famous for speeding down dirt roads and raising clouds of dust. One neighbor asked her, "Miz Wyly, don't you worry about your boys driving so fast?"

"No," she replied. "I can't go with them, so I pray and commit them to the Lord."

She walked courageously through her darkest hour, losing Papa. She taught us that our hope is not in this world but in the one to come, which God promises his children.

She knew Papa was safe at home with the Lord while she was called to carry on. And she did. All of us children saw her get up, love us, care for us, and walk on with grit and good humor.

My Application

As a young girl, I never imagined my life would look so complete. Sometimes in the early days after moving to Amarillo, in our new home, with a lovely new neighborhood, I had to pinch myself to believe I was so happy with so many of my dreams coming true.

Although I had suffered a severe pelvic injury, I had three lovely children. I had risen from the adversity of the Dust Bowl to own land in the same area where my parents bought land in 1929. My husband was successful in his career, highly respected, and preached God's word.

If I had only known what secrets lay right under my nose, the secrets that would shatter my perfect life. I discovered my first clue when I went to his office after we moved to Amarillo.

He needed an address and a phone number he had written on his office notepad. I sat at his desk and looked around for things to tidy up.

In his trash bin, I noticed pieces of a letter. I had never known him to tear up letters. Curious, I fished the pieces out, laid them together, and began reading.

The letter was from an older minister who had mentored Odell. It encouraged him to continue his preaching, to keep his eyes on the Word and the work to be done, and to keep his eyes off the sisters in the congregation. I sat back, trying to take this in.

I was stunned. I wondered, "Was this an issue I needed to address or a general admonition?"

As I lay in bed beside him that night, I wondered if his mind wandered to the pretty ladies of the church. I tried to remember his interactions with the sisters. Nothing made me suspicious.

But I raised a question about his satisfaction in our marriage that made him sit straight up in bed. He hugged and reassured me, seeming almost upset that I would have that question.

I settled my mind, closed my eyes, and willed my heart to settle. Undoubtedly, the church men would see and say something if they suspected him of flirtations.

Later, I saw him being openly flirtatious with a woman! Odell convinced me I was imagining things and then grew angry at my comments. "How can you think such a thing!" was his response. He convinced me that I was unduly jealous.

I thought it odd when a family we knew drove hundreds of miles to make an unannounced and unsolicited visit to Amarillo with their three children. In looking back, it should have been clear to me. The visiting family's wife was seeking emotional support from Odell. The couple returned to their home after staying with us for several days, and I thought nothing more of it. It was just my jealous mind acting up again!

Finally, his sister, a member of our church, became suspicious. She and her husband planned to intercept Odell, and the proof was conclusive.

He was involved with a member of our church. When I found out, I was so angry with him that I threw a glass down the hall one morning as hard as I could. It shattered against his closet at the end of the hall. Two of my children opened their doors, looked in amazement, and then closed them again.

I was astonished, heartsick, and broken as I realized Odell was depending on me throughout his affair to protect our marriage, children, and his reputation. I looked back and saw so many red flags. I should have known something was wrong.

He begged the church and me to forgive him. I knew I would have to forgive him. I decided we could do the arduous work to save our marriage.

I thought I protected our children's faith and church by keeping Odell's problems quiet. The leadership told me to go home and be a good wife, and they would handle the difficult situation.

After years of counseling and prayer, I thought we had reached a better relationship. I knew something was amiss in our marriage, but I didn't know what it was.

I theorized that perhaps his former infidelity still haunted him or me. I sometimes wondered what I could have done differently. Maybe I should have gone with him on all his visits to the needy and the sick.

A few years later, in a new town, ministering at a different church, he seemed emotionally attached to a woman in our congregation. I told him flatly, "Break it off or move out." I assumed he would end the relationship with the other woman. We had worked for years to save our marriage.

For our 32nd anniversary, we went out to eat and looked for a pearl ring. We found one and bought it.

The next evening, Odell sat calmly in the living room and said, "I am moving out. I've already taken my clothes to an apartment I've rented. I'm leaving."

I was shocked. I sat quietly, yet was devastated, and acquiesced to his demands. I asked him if he was sure he wanted to leave.

I have always wondered what he would have done if I had screamed, broken the lamp, or thrown something. Would he have stayed if I pitched a fit right then? Would the outcome have changed if I told him how much I needed him?

I wonder if he wanted more drama from me. To be honest, though, I was tired of fighting for our marriage and Odell's fidelity.

Divorce was my husband's choice. I had worked so hard to carry on normally for the sake of our children. Yet I had sheltered this man whose betrayal was now so blatant. I cried, "Why me?"

I had forgiven him, worked harder on our marriage, and sought godly counseling. This took long months of prayer, self-examination, and work.

I felt humiliated and betrayed. I thought I had been a good wife, yet my efforts failed to save our marriage. I battled self-doubt. I thought he was working as hard as I was to save our marriage, but I was wrong. I had looked at life through rose-colored glasses.

My upbringing did little to prepare me for the lies Odell told me. As I look back, I see that there were so many puzzle pieces that didn't make sense. I had believed his rebukes when he told me my suspicions shocked and hurt him.

Then I considered this world and saw the devastation divorce wreaked on our nation. I finally came to the critical point of saying, "Why **not** me? Why should I be free of suffering?" My misery was not as important as my response.

At about 52, I had a knee replacement. I compare my broken knee to the shattered heart I suffered before and throughout the divorce. The knee came after the heart, but both challenged my spirit.

The first thing I realized was that my knee was not working as it once did, and my marriage wasn't working well. I denied that anything was seriously wrong. But the problem returned with a vengeance, and my husband's attention again wandered. At other times, he seemed better, so I went on with my life.

My knee gave out gradually. Occasionally, I needed a cane to negotiate stairs, but it worked. Similarly, my husband and I had many tough talks, but I thought my marriage would last. My church upbringing trained me to be a sweet and trusting wife. Unfortunately, some of that training prevented me from responding to Odell appropriately.

Early in the marriage, little things I did made him strangely angry. He would not tell me what upset him but expected me to read his mind. He might sulk for several days. Then he would wake up sweet as pie one morning, acting as if nothing had happened.

I did all I could to keep the trauma from our children. And I hoped he would surely do the right thing.

My knee acted up again. Finally, I decided I needed to see a doctor. He found I did indeed have a problem. He gave me shots in the joint, which made it better for a time. As my husband and I went through counseling, I thought the marriage would heal and be okay. I held onto the dream of "Come, grow old with me."

I forgave him, as I knew Jesus had forgiven me. Forgiveness based on Jesus requires intentionality and watchfulness because my heart sometimes wanted to have a pity party. Yet I knew holding onto bitterness would not help my healing and could harm my children and closest friends.

We were working on it, right? I reassured myself with this thought during the disintegration of my knee and my marriage.

The irritation returned. I started limping more. Things could not go on like this, but what would I do? So, I waited. The same happened in my marriage. I waited.

Eventually, the doctor said it was time for surgery. The divorce also happened quickly, right as I mistakenly thought we were about to get past our painful years.

Both the divorce and my knee caused excruciating agony. Dreams are always destroyed in a divorce, expectations of things that will never be. I wished I could go to sleep and finish the entire process—I did not want to see anybody or face another day.

The same with my knee operation. I wanted to sleep till the pain was gone. But after knee surgery, those in charge got me up to walk the next day.

I felt the same during the divorce. I was broken-hearted. People encouraged me and offered sympathy, but I was deeply embarrassed. The shame I felt was intense. Yet broken inside, I immediately resumed my regular workdays at the Texas Department of Human Services.

Blessings are disguised by pain. Going to work was painful, but the distraction was a blessing. My colleagues did not know how badly my heart hurt. Even going to church was hard, but the fellowship was a blessing. Seeing old friends was painful, but their loving comfort was a blessing. Odell was asked to leave the church, and a couple who were among our best friends came over to share that the announcement was tastefully and tearfully made.

I slowly and reluctantly began to put weight on the wounded knee and went to physical therapy. Similarly, during my divorce, I had to keep working and seeing people, although I was in a fog of pain. And waves of pain didn't always hit at the best times. Sometimes as I walked into a meeting, I had to choke back tears.

Recovering from the divorce, I kept up a healing routine of walking every evening. I sought out counseling, which I found helpful. Understanding what I had been through from an emotional and mental perspective was essential in moving on. But there was no magic pill to make the pain go away. Out of necessity, I moved on with my life, just as Mama had after the death of Papa.

A few weeks after my knee surgery, I noticed my knee supported me. I slowly began to put one foot in front of the other. More days passed, and I was walking—slowly and laboriously, but walking.

The divorce recovery was the same. The first few weeks felt terrible. But after a few months, I could go almost all day without thinking about my sorrows. Healing takes time.

Using a walker, then a cane for balance, the discomfort was gone, and my knee felt better than it had in a long time. I began to enjoy the freedom of walking pain-free. During the divorce process, accepting the support of well-meaning friends, co-workers and relatives made a difference. But, like physical therapy, seeing others was something I had to make myself do.

My ex-husband's brother and his wife came over. They offered support. I pointed out that my ex-husband needed their help even more than I did because he was losing his job, church family, and the esteem of a wide circle of friends. They reluctantly agreed to offer him their support.

I tried not to talk about my pain and the divorce except to a trusted few. I have seen people who focused on their pain and talked about it to anyone who would listen. Too much self-focus is usually a burden for others.

I moved to a sunny apartment and began my life as a 50-something single person. I had an excellent job and spent my vacation days keeping up with my children and grandchildren, with new additions arriving regularly. I traveled to their homes in Texas, Oklahoma, Maine, and Washington and enjoyed all the little ones.

My biggest struggle was the sheer loneliness. After a life that included a house full of people, I ate meals alone and spent evenings after work alone. Yet this restful quiet led to months of new and challenging opportunities.

God showered me with new vistas. In late 1974, I was offered a new position as Volunteer Coordinator for the 40 counties in the Texas Panhandle and the South Plains. I traveled over 65,000 square miles to implement the "Care Corps" initiative, which linked volunteers with the Department of Human Services staff and clients.

I received training in Austin and met young, bright, innovative people. The task was challenging but allowed me to meet community leaders in the Panhandle, true "salt of the earth" servants of their communities.

In Lubbock, I attended Quaker Avenue Church of Christ. Many of the members were lifelong friends. I took time off from work to travel with them. We went to seven European countries, Israel, and Africa. At Namikango Mission in Malawi, Africa, we renewed our friendship with B. and Ruth Shelburne, who ministered there for decades.

Ruth took us to game reserves and on tours of fascinating sights across the beautiful country. The mission site and birthing hospital are an ongoing outreach to the Malawi people we support.

One of our tours took us to the fantastic city of Venice. As our group waited for the next boat taxi, I wandered along the canal's edge. I looked around just in time to see the boat gently edging off the pier. I would rather be soaked than wait alone at the hotel, so I ran and jumped for the boat.

Two brave ladies reached out and pulled me on board. Tommy Langford, my long-time friend, said, "Well, I'd heard of the running broad jump, but now I've seen one!" We all had a good laugh, and I was not very wet.

In 1979, the state of Texas offered me a contract manager position in a new location. My fellowship in Lubbock provided a vast network of support for me. I had leaned on them for encouragement and companionship through the divorce and for many seasons after, and I hated to leave. I wondered whether I could survive the separation from dear friends but used the same principle I employed to survive my divorce: I put one foot in front of the other and kept moving forward.

After moving to Amarillo, I bought a house near a church many old friends attended. God, who is always faithful, provided for my needs. I entertained friends and family in Amarillo and had a cadre of cronies with whom I went to movies and social events.

I enjoyed my single life. Later, the minister told me he didn't know what to do for these ladies, but I came along and ministered to them. I didn't think of them as a ministry but as friends who needed companionship, just as I did.

God gave me helpful people. In my new position, John Noyes trained me to understand the contracts and procedures I needed for my new job. John was a friend of my daughter and son from their high school days. His patience, expertise, and humor helped in this transition. I worked there from 1979 until I retired in 1990.

As I resisted self-pity and slowly let go of my past dreams, God, in mercy and grace, re-invented me as I walked into new roles. When you are down, look for the next thing God presents you, big or small. He is faithful. He will guide you on a steady path.

Get up and travel slowly, deliberately, and intentionally, holding onto God's hand. Don't rush. Wait on Him. He will heal your heart and guide you to retreats of peace and unexpected valleys of blessing.

I realized that Mama's response to the tragedy in her life modeled my desire to make good choices. As devastating as my divorce was, I knew my response to the situation was more important than the circumstances.

Scriptures to Consider

Brothers, as an example of patience in the face of suffering, take the prophets who spoke in the name of the Lord. As you know, we consider blessed those who have persevered. You have heard of Job's perseverance and have seen what the Lord finally brought about. The Lord is full of compassion and mercy. James 5:10-11

1. Share the story of Job's suffering with one another. Why does James say he is our example? What situation has caused you a long season of suffering?
2. Which biblical character encourages you the most?

The Missing Conversation *from Mevanee*

I thought I lived the perfect childhood. I couldn't imagine a more ideal family. My dad was highly respected and sought after as a preacher. We enjoyed many sunny days together, camping and boating. My mom made home a haven.

I noticed that when Dad was moody, the atmosphere at home changed, but I didn't know what to make of it, much less how to address it. Now I know so much was going on beneath the surface.

I married Phill Parmer, my high school sweetheart, in 1971. We moved to LSU for graduate school, and on a 1974 visit to Lubbock to see my parents, my mother confided that my dad had "woman trouble (she paused) - again."

What? AGAIN? I never knew about any of his problems and Mom's struggles to sustain the marriage until that August afternoon of 1974.

Like my mother, I guess I was too naïve. My older brother knew about Dad's problem, but my younger brother and I did not. My best friends had known, and everyone thought someone else would tell me. No one had that conversation, not with me.

My mother explained that she thought I knew. She protected us because the elders told her to go home and do her best. She felt that meant carrying on as though nothing had happened. She thought that the knowledge of our dad's affair could shipwreck our faith, as we were all in our teens. So, that was a conversation that did not happen.

Truly, my mother is a wise woman. Parents today often do not consider the long-term effects of their words and actions.

She protected us from the stress and harm that our dad created. He had counted on her to do the right thing.

Phill and I drove back to Baton Rouge, and he comforted me while I cried. Over the next few months, I tried to process everything. I felt like I was continually waking up in a nightmare.

I had to reassess all my dad stood for and taught us. This re-evaluation of my faith was a blessing. The perfect childhood I thought I remembered was an illusion, but the faith I learned in my church was not. I held tight to the truth.

Within a month, Mom called to say Dad had moved out. Counselors told my mother that with Dad's personality type, whatever that was, he probably always enjoyed a hidden life. And he likely had many more affairs than she knew. Were his problem sins, mental illness, or both?

My older brother Ira, his wife Linda, Phill, and I spoke with Dad at Thanksgiving following his move to an apartment. He seemed shocked that we were upset he was leaving Mom.

We pleaded with him to reconsider his actions. We left his dark apartment, Linda sobbing uncontrollably. I watched her and thought, "I should be sobbing, too," but I was in shock. Unbelievably, as we left, Dad invited us to his wedding, oblivious to our pain.

My Grandmother Wyly told Mother, "Of all my children, I thought your marriage was the strongest." So I wasn't just imagining their strong relationship. I am guessing my dad knew how to make things look good, even to my perceptive grandmother. But sadly, his secret life, untreated depression, sin, and self-pity led to massive self-deception.

My dad helped hundreds of people come to faith. I know Satan draws a big bullseye on the backs of all who live for the Lord, especially those in leadership. And Satan will strike at opportune times, repeatedly.

I know God ultimately protects us when we walk closely with Him. "Be self-controlled and alert. Your enemy the devil prowls around like a roaring lion looking for someone to devour. Resist him, standing firm in the faith, because you know that your brothers throughout the world are undergoing the same kind of sufferings." I Peter 5:8-9

When Dad left our family, I wondered painfully why my brothers and I were not important enough for him to want to stay with us. We were all newly married, just starting on exciting paths.

Didn't he want to know his future grandchildren? Didn't he want to see us all grow in our faith? Didn't he want to give us help and advice as we navigated parenting, leaving us a legacy of faith that would endure through generations?

His mental state was not healthy. Satan, the deceiver, hit his mark, and sin had done its damage. That understanding does not erase the deep pain of losing my dad or the shame of knowing he hurt many people who loved him. I visited him with my family during our annual holiday trips to Texas from Champaign, Illinois. Those awkward talks reminded me he was not the father I thought I grew up loving and knowing.

My dad passed on February 17, 2012, just before his 88th birthday. He died from injuries sustained in a car accident in Lubbock in November of 2011. His heart was not strong enough to allow recovery. I last spoke to him in December 2011 in the rehabilitation home. Although he was affectionate, and I had forgiven him, I no longer trusted his words.

I sat in 1991 surrounded by my eight beloved grandchildren. I have traveled to spend time with them since their births. They are a constant source of amazement and joy. Back row L-R: Elizabeth Purdy Evans, Sydney Purdy Sexton, Dell Purdy, Penelope Parmer Westwater, Cory Parmer, Shannon Parmer Butler. Front row L-R: Jonathan Purdy, Nova Wyly Purdy, Rebecca Purdy Eads. Now, they are busy with their own families.

Upon arriving in Kenya, our group of missionaries, teachers, and visitors drove north to Kitale, crossing the Great Rift Valley, home to various animals and plants. My photograph below captures an elephant family under an acacia tree at Masai Mara near Oloololo Escarpment in March 1994.

Lesson 6

**I learned in Africa
that we are very wealthy and privileged
in these United States, full of opportunities.**

My mother's example also served me well in retirement. When she moved from her farm in Deaf Smith County to Friona, a small town nearby, she stayed active and on the move.

She planted a bodacious garden and canned much of her food, as she had on the farm. Baking a pie and cake every week, she was often the first to deliver food to families during illness, death, or a welcomed birth. She looked for ways to encourage others every day. From reading her journals, it is clear she battled loneliness and looked forward to visitors.

She cared for several families' young children in town and babysat for her grandchildren regularly. One winter, she spent the whole school year in South Dakota caring for my niece Crista while my sister Myrtice taught school.

My children loved it when Odell and I held gospel meetings out of town because Grandma Wyly came to tend them. They remembered her nursing them through the mumps while we were gone.

She advised her sons in their farming ventures and listened to all her children. She wrote letters to her grandchildren and took them on road trips to visit one another. She was the glue that kept our family close throughout her lifetime.

When she saw that she needed more monthly income, she bought a house and had it moved to the back of her lot to rent. She was always involved with her renters, helping them however she could. She saw needs and took action to meet them.

Along with my mother, Margaret Williams was another inspiration in my retirement. She had retired from teaching and became my housemate in Lubbock, which was quite an unexpected blessing right after my divorce. When the opportunity arose, she traveled to Africa to teach the missionaries' children at Namikango Mission in Malawi.

Her work foreshadowed my later opportunities in Africa. She sent me long letters detailing her delightful time, instructing her young students and explaining the culture. Her introduction to daily African life through her correspondence made my decisions easier.

My Application

Approaching retirement, I was unsure what lay ahead, but I knew I would not sit in a rocker and knit as others might expect. At one of our church meetings with visiting missionaries we supported, I met Susan Hayes, a young mother serving in Kenya looking for a teacher for her children.

She and her husband worked in a compound with three other families with kindergarteners and first graders. I knew the older parents of some of the missionaries and had heard about the excellent work this group was doing.

Susan asked, and I jumped at the opportunity. This was the perfect retirement adventure I was looking for. My daughter Mevanee and her family were already in Johannesburg doing mission work, and I knew I could travel to South Africa to visit them. Their mission point was urban, mine was rural.

I flew to Africa and rented a small colonial cottage that became a children's schoolhouse. I improvised, and we all had quite a time. I still receive news from them today as adults.

I had seen my mother raise seven children using her imagination and resources to keep life stable under challenging circumstances.

I didn't have as many resources in Africa as a classroom in modern America, but I had watched Mama enrich our lives with her ingenuity. We made puppets out of materials on hand and shared reading materials. Children always enjoy dress-up occasions, so we had a crazy hair day and a promotion day with graduation gowns.

What a fascinating time to be in Africa! As a necessity, I hired a yardman, a house girl, and a nightguard. I had never employed household help in the States. The people of Kenya are patient, kind, and giving, although their lives are difficult.

On chilly mornings, Stephen, the yardman, came in and built a fire in the fireplace. The six children and I loved to sit in the warmth and read.

African culture is different in unexpected and interesting ways. Some men have more than one wife. This leads to problems because usually, the first wife assumes the primary role (she's the boss of the other wives), and the second wife often feels slighted. Also, the first-born child is treated with deference and receives the most significant inheritance. Other children are likely to resent this favoritism. Having one wife is vastly less complicated than having two or more.

The food, ugali (pronounced like oo-golly), a cornmeal mush, is a staple in the diet of most Kenyans. The sparsely stocked store shelves starkly contrasted with our standards in America, where shelves bulged with goods. I grew used to simpler food and added some of my favorites. The menu reminded me of my childhood diet. Kiosks offered snacks, but we prepared most meals from scratch. Mexican food was rarely available, but I enjoyed making taco salad.

Judith, my house girl, watched one day as I prepared a whole chicken I had bought that day at the market. It was plucked and cleaned. After cutting it into pieces to cook, I asked her to put the entrails, feet, and neck in the trash. She asked for what I was about to throw away.

She went to her small home at the back of the lot and made a meal out of it. The next day her husband stopped by on his way to work and said, "Thank you for the chicken dinner." What I considered waste made a meal for Judith's family.

I saw love and knowledge of God's Word break down racial and cultural barriers. When we went to the villages for church, the singing was lively, and the prayers were heartfelt. Sometimes, we met in a simple church building and sometimes under a tree.

Once a snake crawled along the wall during a sermon. While everyone paused, one of the men got up and killed it. Then, the lesson resumed.

I drove to town in a mission vehicle to complete errands. Once I arrived, 10 or 12 young street boys gathered around me, asking for money. I knew they were going to buy gasoline to sniff.

I told them to meet me at the bakery. They waited quietly and sat on a low rock fence alongside the bakery. I bought loaves of light bread, like Mama used to make, and gave each one several pieces. Many people in Africa live in poverty and need daily help.

Every day, I learned more about the customs and habits of the diverse Kenyan culture. Even the way they shake hands is different. The people have two names: an "English" name, which is usually biblical, and their proper Kenyan name, which is given at birth. I learned basic Swahili phrases from my household members. The learning curve was steep but enjoyable. My season in Africa gave me beautiful memories from a surprising setting. Life was full of *National Geographic* experiences and sights in Kenya. Besides my huge British garden, I visited rain forests, the famous Maasai Mara National Reserve, native villages, and markets.

Kitale is in western Kenya, near Uganda. I grew up on a farm, raising garden vegetables and wheat with cows, horses, pigs, and chickens, which is remarkably similar to the farms in the Kitale area. I thoroughly enjoyed the setting and the people.

My upbringing in our simple house on the prairie prepared me well for Africa. Most Africans in Kitale lived in homes like the one where I grew up: no electricity, running water, or indoor bathroom. Although the accommodation was not as luxurious as Westerners expected in the 1990s, I had running cold and hot water, electricity, and refrigeration in my colonial cottage.

Africa provided a beautiful yard with cannas, Bird of Paradise, banana trees, and other exotic flowers and trees. What a treat for a woman from the Panhandle of Texas!

Scriptures to Consider

Listen, my beloved brothers: Has not God chosen the poor of this world to be rich in faith and to inherit the kingdom He promised those who love Him? James 2:5

1. Sometimes, we pity people who live in third-world countries. What does James indicate in these verses?

2. How might we reconsider our values? As a very wealthy nation, how do we need to align ourselves?

God's Grace for Mom *from Mevanee*

Once, after the divorce, my mother asked me if I was going to be okay. I said, "Yes, I'll be okay, IF you're okay." I did not mean to put more pressure on her, but I guess I inadvertently did.

I had seen God work in her life to always go beyond what anyone expected. While we lived in Haltom City, she commuted with a group of ladies working on degrees at Texas Women's University in Denton, Texas. She completed her Bachelor of Science in Home Economics in 1972, about the same time Ira, Linda, Phill, and I were completing degrees. But she took 170 hours for her B. S.! She had taken extra courses just for fun while waiting for her carpool to finish their classes. She preferred to keep busy rather than waste the hours.

I worried about Mom and wondered how God would take care of her. Over the next few years, His hand was evident. I could hear with a boom, "I have been with her all her life, and I will be with her now." Since then, we have had many good talks about God's care for her during and after the divorce.

I saw God's grace for my mother immediately as the painful process of healing began. Mom received unexpected promotions in her jobs and lane changes that challenged her, required increased time, and gave her more income.

Church friends stepped up to offer comfort and friendship. She also had wonderful retreats and took tours with Quaker Avenue Church of Christ in Lubbock to Europe, the Holy Lands, and Africa. I felt that after the divorce was passed and healing occurred, she blossomed in wonderful opportunities only a loving Father can provide. He redeemed her pain in beautiful ways.

As Volunteer Coordinator for the top 40 counties in the Panhandle, Mom traveled long hours and met many hard-working people. She did not move into a position with history — the job was newly created. No one in the department was sure about her job description, but they picked the right person.

Mom believes you should earn every penny, and she willingly worked long hours, driving thousands of miles. She considered it a gift from God, a sure provision from Him socially, emotionally, and financially. Incredibly, she had more surprises.

She applied for and received a new position in Amarillo, moved to Amarillo, and was surrounded by friends at Anna Street Church of Christ. She had known some of those dear people since childhood.

After I moved with my family to Africa in 1986, she visited us with her cousin Glenna and later with Phill's mother, Mama Lorna. Of course, when she worked in Kenya, she could "come by" Johannesburg, which was a tremendous encouragement to me.

God blessed Mom with a stronger faith, great jobs, more income, loving communities, trips with friends, a ministry at Anna Street Church of Christ, and great fun in retirement. Returning from her first African teaching experience, she became a member of the board of the Christian Relief Fund. Her renewal of old friendships as she served on the board led to more blessings than we could have ever guessed.

I loved my year teaching in Africa. My beautiful students were Karissa, Benjamin, and Ryan on the left. I'm holding Ty while Kathryn, Kyle, and Noah are on the right. I had grown up in a two-room school for 8 grades, so I enjoyed having all the children together. The photograph captures my going-away party in June of 1991, and the children gave me a lovely necklace.

I returned from Africa and served on the Christian Relief Fund board. There, I met a friend from my past, Ken Vaughn. After "going around together" for over a year, we picked a date. On our wedding day, Ken pinned a flower on my lapel.

Little did I know how many adventures Ken and I would share together! God brought us amazing blessings through many people across continents and over twenty years together.

Lesson 7

Be a little venturesome, and enjoy your whole life!

Our school term in Kitale ended, and I flew from Kenya to Amarillo in June of 1991. My daughter-in-law, Linda Purdy, asked me to serve on the board of the Christian Relief Fund. I felt honored to help this wonderful organization, which sponsors children in poverty worldwide.

At my first meeting, I met an acquaintance from the past, Ken Vaughn. In 1945, Ken attended a Bible Reading in Fort Worth, Texas, taught by G. B. Shelburne and N. L. Clark. He was an 18-year-old single young man. I was newly married to Odell Purdy. The young students gave sermons, and I remembered Ken's attempt made more sense than most of the sermons of the aspiring preachers who presented that month.

He later married Nova Russell. Yes, Ken was married to two Novas! Ken's children lovingly referred to us as Nova 1 and Nova 2. Ken and Nova 1 lived in El Paso for several years and moved to Irving, Texas. They had five children, all grown by 1991. His daughters Susan and Deb became friends with my daughter Mevanee when we moved to Fort Worth in 1968. Ken's sons are David, Kenny, and Mark, remarkable men.

Ken had served on the board since the beginning of the Christian Relief Fund. His wife had suffered from a long illness and died while I was in Africa.

After renewing our friendship during the Christian Relief Fund Board meetings throughout 1991, Ken had heart surgery. I called him and wished him well. During my 18 years of being single, I had never considered men or dating again. Marriage was certainly not on my radar. But shortly after my phone call, we started "going around together."

Ken asked me to marry him in the summer of 1992. I told him, "You don't even know me, not really!"

He responded, "I know enough."

I didn't give him an answer until November, after I took him to visit Mevanee and her family, who had moved to Champaign, Illinois. After the visit and her approval, I told him on the flight home, "If your offer of marriage is still good, I think I'll take you up on that."

He responded with a broad smile, "Then I'll be the happiest man in the DFW airport." Dell Purdy relates a story in his tribute to Ken at the end of this book. Our casual marriage announcement caused quite a stir at the Purdy Thanksgiving table.

We selected December 28, 1992, as the day in the next month. We had been "going around together" for almost a year.

All our stateside children attended, and our special musical friends, *Rejoice*, sang. Karen Talley, Joyce Loe, Pat Greenwood, and Lilly Rogers shared, "There's a Sweet, Sweet Spirit in this Place." And there was!

It was beautiful and simple. Our grandchildren had great fun painting the cake topper, so the bride and groom had white hair. My cousin Glenna, with whom I had shared my first wedding, came and brought some of her children and grandchildren.

I had no idea how Ken and I complemented each other. He loved to talk, and I loved to listen. We enjoyed people and offering simple hospitality, yet we liked our quiet space. We enjoyed keeping many friends and family for days or weeks.

Thankfully, we both enjoyed traveling. Our children were spread all over the United States. He owned a timeshare, so we used our credit to travel.

We enjoyed our eight children and their families when they came or invited us to come. They were all congenial, so we rejoiced in their visits. None of them lived with us after our marriage, so "blending" them was easy.

I remember the first time Ken and I disagreed. I had been waiting for the other foot to drop, as it always did in my first marriage. Or waiting for the "long sulk." But no! Ken wasn't upset with me, and we sat down and discussed our problems. What a big difference and a blessing!

The biggest surprise was how God used us in Africa. Of course, I shared my enlightening experiences in Kenya with Ken. He was also knowledgeable about several missionaries in Africa and was especially close to one of them, Shawn Tyler. His church in Irving had supported Shawn and Linda's work through the years.

On a furlough from his work in Kenya, Shawn surprised us by asking Ken to help supervise the construction of Messiah Theological Institute in Kitale, Kenya.

I taught there two years earlier and loved the missionaries, their families, and the Kenyan families I had come to know.

Shawn assured Ken that the Africans especially respected those with white hair. He would supervise a team of builders who would see his white hair and think, "There's a man with great wisdom!" Ken chuckled when he heard that.

Shawn explained more. He said Ken's expertise in supervising the budget and the building would be invaluable. It would also free up Shawn to devote more time to the ministry of the word and prayer.

At our granddaughter, Elizabeth Evans, wedding, Ken and I recorded our marriage advice for future generations in an old-fashioned photographer's booth. We wrote our simple guidelines on the side.

Have fun – if it ain't fun, don't do it.

Sometimes you just have to agree to disagree.

Kiss + make up.

You, too, will be old someday. Have fun all the way!

Through years of serving in Kenya, Shawn is one of the most skilled evangelists in Africa. He knows the language, the people and how to communicate God's word across cultures.

We knew serving with Shawn would be a joy. So, after consulting with our families and closest friends, we joyfully accepted this new challenge.

Ken was perfect for Africa. In addition to having incredible patience and humility, he could fix almost anything—and many things in Africa need "fixing."

Ken's long career in many departments at Sears served well in preparing him for Africa. He worked in everything from outdoor sales to the automotive department. He kept his children's cars running and worked on plumbing and general house repairs. He even restored a deck at Mevanee's house, which lost its foundation due to rotted wood.

He said, "Go get carjacks. And if you have two, bring them both." He and his helpers jacked up the deck, found the problem, and installed a new beam.

Ken should have been an engineer. Indeed, all three of his sons, David, Kenny, and Mark, became engineers. He only finished high school but was the valedictorian of his class.

The Hayes family, who lived in the compound near Shawn and his wife Linda, returned to the United States for a brief visit. They contacted Carol Montgomery in Memphis to teach the children I had taught two years before and asked me to teach again. With the Hayes family, Carol, Ken, and I flew back to Kitale in 1993.

As we drove from Nairobi to Kitale, Ken was awed by the countryside, the little villages, and the wildlife of the Great Rift Valley.

He said, "I have heard the missionaries' reports and seen their pictures, but you must be here. What incredible differences between our lifestyle [in the States] and the reality for these people: the primitive construction in the villages, the sweeping savannahs with herds of eland, the goats on the road." And he chuckled at the herd of goats inconveniently blocking our path and their absurd antics.

The manicured garden made our beautiful home in Kitale, Kenya, a tropical paradise. Carol and I taught in the "little red schoolhouse" on the far left.

We found an old bathtub in the yard, scrubbed it clean, and put pillows in it. The kids sat in the tub and read as a reward for finishing their work.

Ken became the principal, with an emphasis on the *pal*. The children viewed him as their friend. At Christmas, he played Santa Claus and dressed up as the famous bunny at Easter. His performances delighted the children.

He also supervised the new building site, the Messiah Theological Institute. The workers noted Ken's white hair. They got him a chair for comfort, and subsequently, they called him "The **Chair**-man."

Because Carol was a kindergarten specialist, I taught the second, third, and fourth graders whom I had taught two years before and enjoyed so much.

When Carol taught the kindergarteners and first graders the ABCs, she took photographs all over Kitale of items that began with each letter. She pasted the pictures into a scrapbook to help the children learn their alphabet.

Carol was young and energetic. She had just completed a degree in early childhood education and significantly contributed to the students' education. I loved our collaboration.

The African reckoning of time suited Ken. Compared to most Americans, he was very patient. He waited in long lines to get building blueprints approved or visas processed. I wrote in a 1990s letter to Mevanee:

> Ken has gone to town for the 5th time to see about getting our work permits. First, he got the forms—then he went 3 times yesterday. They never tell you what all is needed, "Oh, you also need a letter from your employer."
>
> You say, "Here is one."
>
> They say, "But it must be on your organization's letterhead."
>
> You get that, with copies of passport pictures, resumes, a letter from the Amarillo police to prove you have no criminal record, a marriage license to prove "this woman belongs to you," a letter from our minister, church, etc., etc., and they say, "You have to buy one of our pink folders." So you go to another long line, buy one, put it all in the folder, and take it back.
>
> Then they say, "We must see your passport."
>
> So you say, "But I supposed the copies and pictures would suffice."
>
> And they say, "No, we must see your original passport."
>
> So, Ken is making a list of what is needed for the future use of other missionaries. But they already say new missionaries must also have an ordination certificate from their sponsoring church.

Ken never flinched or seemed put out by the endless waiting or new requirements. His standard response was, "Okay, we can do that." He learned patience long before he came to Africa.

We returned to Texas in June 1994 after our nine-month school term. We had some decisions to make that we hadn't settled since we were married and had made the whirlwind trip to Kenya. Ken owned a home in Irving, Texas, between Fort Worth and Dallas, and I owned a home in Amarillo. We hadn't decided which area functioned best as our permanent residence and had no reason to rush into a decision.

During a trip to Fort Worth in the summer's heat, Ken came in from working in the yard and said, "I think we should move to Amarillo, where it's not so hot and humid."

We got stuck several times in Irving's long lines of traffic. That "sealed the deal" for Ken. He was ready to relocate to Amarillo, so we bought a new home together in Puckett Place, a southwest Amarillo neighborhood.

Surprisingly, in 1997, a church in Abilene, Texas, contacted us. A situation had arisen calling for their staff to return to the U.S. from a downtown mission in Kampala, Uganda. We were both eager to spend more time in Africa because we immensely enjoyed Kenya's people and beauty. After interviewing several couples, the committee selected us to go. It was, I think, because we could pay our way there and needed no salary!

In January 1998, we returned to Kampala, Africa, to serve for a year. Our purpose was to stabilize the church without its American leaders.

Our first home overlooked Lake Victoria, providing a beautiful view. The work differed significantly from Kitale in Kenya, a rural town surrounded by garden farms. Kampala, by contrast, was a bustling metropolis, and we enjoyed both places.

Topista, our house girl in Kampala, was well-trained by former missionaries. She was small, middle-aged, and spoke

English. She lived in a small room in a building behind our house. She came in every morning at eight to cook and clean.

Ken usually rose before I did and often brought me coffee in bed. Topista thought this was highly improper. She told me she believed I should serve my husband as the lady of the house, not vice versa. Secretly, however, she wished she could have just such a serving husband.

One day, she sat quietly in the back seat on the way to town. Then she asked, "Mr. Ken, have you ever thought of taking another wife?" In Africa, it was common practice for a man to have two or three wives.

I answered quickly for him. Now, I wish I had kept quiet to hear what he would have said, or if he could have phrased a quick repartee. Would he have blushed, trying to frame a response?

But I immediately said, "I would not permit that." Ken's answer would have been, perhaps, more kind.

Once, Topista made a special request that we take her relative, sick with AIDS, back out to her farm to die. The woman was in her 30s. We drove down an unpaved alley in town to pick her up. People hung their wash beside the narrow tracks and were not happy we were stirring up dust, especially at the end, where a cul-de-sac forced us to make a 180-degree turn.

The ailing woman came out to our car. She wanted to be at her farm, which she said was large. We asked her, "How big is your farm?"

"A whole acre," she responded. Half the village people waited to meet us when we arrived at the farm. They gently unloaded the lady with AIDS. Shortly after we delivered her home, she passed.

She was literally "gathered to her people," like the patriarchs in the Old Testament. The loss of people due to AIDS persisted throughout the decade we worked in Africa. Tragically, the disease has decimated the continent.

I shared some time every week with a group of women, most of whom helped raise children orphaned by the AIDS epidemic in their extended families.

School fees were a heavy burden for most of these families. I told them about an American organization that sponsored orphans and helped families with school fees, food, and medical care.

One woman shook her head, doubting that such help existed. Her disbelief made me determined. I called the Christian Relief Fund, discussed the details, and asked if they could sponsor a group of orphans in Kampala. Linda Purdy, my daughter-in-law, Baxter Loe, and the CRF staff were eager to help.

The Christian Relief Fund only required a list of children, describing each one and their families' stories and each child's photograph. Later, we recruited a young man from Kampala to administer this work.

We flew back to the States at the end of the year, only to return to Kampala a few years later. Ken continued to supervise new building construction. The sponsored children from the program, which I started before leaving, greeted us with great enthusiasm. One even bowed before us. I lifted her and told her we were not their benefactors, that other people in America supported them.

One lady explained that this girl was part of a large refugee family. Her CRF support provided enough food to feed her whole family. I was thankful to be a small part of starting this good work.

Adding to the AIDS problem, governments across central Africa were unstable, causing refugees to flee their homelands due to extreme danger. Refugee camps existed near the borders of many countries. Whichever tribe had power in the government favored their group above others, which caused enormous problems for those not in power. Sadly, the situation has not changed for many African nations. Tribalism still rips the fabric of the continent.

While in Kampala, I noticed an extensive collection of books sent from the churches around Abilene, Texas. The books spilled messily over several rooms.

Although I'm not a librarian by training, I set up the books, arranging them by general subject and the author's last name. When I came in the following day, my busy helper, who had arrived earlier, had begun rearranging the books according to height!

I decided the more straightforward the organization, the better. I explained to the facilities manager that we would arrange our resources alphabetically by author and group them generally by broad categories. Our work progressed slowly but methodically until we had some idea of the location of the materials our patrons requested.

We used a simple numbering system and began lending books for a small deposit. When our reader returned the book, we refunded the deposit. As far as I know, ours was the only lending library in Uganda.

Once, a couple at church invited Ken and me to their wedding. Topista "braided" my white locks, and I wore an appropriately bright African dress. The ceremony was joyful and full of unusual customs, which we Americans immensely enjoyed.

Watching Ken serve in Africa was a joy. We both loved the culture, and his skill set suited the needs well.

My Application

Many people in Africa are like my mother, Alta Wyly, as they work hard and resourcefully in the face of overwhelming difficulties. They do not grumble or complain about their inconveniences or tragedies.

Mama worked hard well into her eighties. Her love of spontaneity showed throughout her life. Once, when we children were young, she had my oldest brother drive her across the fields to a barnstorming pilot who took her up for an airplane ride. She thought the $1 fee was worth the excitement of flying.

Mama was a little venturesome her whole life and enjoyed having a car that excited her grandchildren. At 71 years old, she traded her 1961 Galaxie for a new 1964 Galaxie 500XL. It was a beautiful turquoise with a black pleated interior. Its 390 Thunderbird engine was not a "Granny" car.

Mama prepared me well to enjoy my entire life. She clearly enjoyed people and welcomed adventures, which enriched our lives.

I think Mama would have enjoyed Africa. I consider it a privilege to have lived among the African people. I found it motivating to help someone with minimal forethought and effort daily. Sharing a meal or a few coins helped open opportunities for these humble, gentle, and patient people. And the Africans expressed gratitude for even my smallest generosity.

As I meditate on these seven lessons life taught me, I thank my Mama for showing me how to turn from tragedy to a new future. She did that even after the staggering loss of Papa. Her courage showed me how to walk faithfully through the hard years of my marriage and find my new direction.

She did good things for us children and for the people who populated those dusty acres in Deaf Smith County, Texas. We children saw her determination to be a giver, not a taker.

She stayed active and lived a life of value and balance through her later years. Even as I aged, I found her example an abundant blessing.

Scriptures to Consider

But the wisdom that comes from heaven is first of all pure; then peace-loving, considerate, submissive, full of mercy and good fruit, impartial and sincere. Peacemakers who sow in peace raise a harvest of righteousness. James 3:17

1. In what ways did this heavenly wisdom bless Alta's life and then Nova's, as well?

2. Which qualities of heavenly wisdom do you most desire to cultivate in your life?

After we returned from Africa, Ken and I enjoyed many beautiful trips. We attended church conferences, visited old friends, rocked new grandbabies, and even cruised to Alaska. Below, we pose for a photograph on an Alaskan cruise.

> When evening comes, there will be light.
> Zechariah 14:7

Whatever poet, orator, or sage
May say of it, old age is still old age.
It is the waning, not the crescent moon;
The dusk of evening, not the blaze of noon . . . .

What then? Shall we sit idly down and say
The night hath come; it is no longer day?
The night hath not yet come; we are not quite
Cut off from labor by the falling light;
Something remains for us to do or dare;
Even the oldest tree some fruit may bear . . . .

For age is opportunity no less
Than youth itself, though in another dress,
And as the evening twilight fades away
The sky is filled with stars, invisible by day.

--from *Morituri Salutamus*
   [We Who Are About to Die Salute You]
   Henry Wadsworth Longfellow

This famous scripture and poetry excerpt was displayed in an old clock on Nova's wall. As she aged, she indeed found abundant opportunities to bless others.

Mevanee and I paused after church at Central Church of Christ in Amarillo for a photo. We did not know it at the time, but it would be one of our last visits there together. COVID 19 closed church for several months, and my waning strength prevented me from getting out of the house in the following years. We were so grateful the church offered virtual services online for years and was ready for the challenges of the pandemic.

Epilogue

September 2024

I slow down my schedule and sit with Mom. These last two years with her have been the hardest. My heart feels heavy with the gradual loss and grief that she is not her active, social, clear-minded, book-reading self.

She can't see or hear like she could in 2020. She says the television presenters talk too fast. Lately, she's been sleeping 20 hours a day. Caregivers say that sleep is a blessing. But I miss her.

She remembers Ken with gratitude, and all her children and grandchildren are grateful for their 22 years together. Ken was a mighty good man, we all agree. His children are dear friends.

After their service in Kampala, Uganda, in 1997, Ken returned to Africa for a few months to supervise building projects with Shawn Tyler. Mom stayed home. Mom and Ken loved the work there, but she couldn't take the rigors of walking on her bad knee.

On February 22, 2005, Abilene Christian University honored Ken and Nova at the Halbert Institute for Missions, the annual Lectureship, for their contributions to mission work and spreading the gospel in Africa. Almost all their children were there to share the joy.

Ken and Mom regularly offered hospitality to many, hosting small Bible study groups and entertaining their children, grandchildren, and friends.

They traveled to beautiful locations, including Lake Tahoe, Pagosa Springs, Colorado, and family reunions. Generous as ever, they invited friends and relatives to join them. They enjoyed their treks until 2013, when Ken struggled with his energy level.

In January 2014, the doctor diagnosed Ken with myelofibrosis, and his daughter Susan came to Amarillo to help with his care. Family reunions celebrated him, and visitors came right to the end. He passed on to his reward on September 20, 2014.

At his memorial service, Dell Purdy, one of his step-grandsons, gave a moving tribute, which he allowed us to share at the end of this book.

A few days later, Mother celebrated her 90th birthday. As we sat eating lunch, she recited the following poem to me:

> These things chiefly do I desire —
> To bake and sew and make a fire,
> A garden plot to plant and tend,
> The frequent visits of a friend,
> Long, useful years with joys to share,
> Health to life's end,
> Home, calm, faith, prayer. *Author unknown*

I had never heard it before, but I held it in my heart, pondering whether to move to Amarillo so she could live out her remaining years, fulfilling the chief desires listed above. I thought about her life and what it would look like as her eyesight failed. Sorting out her bookshelves, I found a small photo album, giving me more to consider.

Over ten young women in Kenya and East Africa collected their photographs in an album as a thank-you gift to Mom. She spoke to them at a retreat, and they each wrote a note of thanks on the back of their sweet pictures. Her impact on them and their esteem for her teaching made coming to live with her a sure choice.

In 2015, after we both retired from teaching, my husband Phill and I moved from Champaign, Illinois. We said we would all try to live temporarily in her Amarillo home for a year. Later, we decided to make the move permanent.

Mom sold her Puckett Place residence, and we moved in together, where she has a large master suite. Our lives together consisted of 5% care and 95% normal activities. Her loss of sight required only a little assistance. She was not happy when, in 2016, she lost her driver's license entirely.

When Phill and I moved in with her, I read and reread what I had written from Duane's version aloud. She usually added more to the story and found some writings by her siblings to include in the memoir.

We visited relatives in Hereford and Friona and made a video at the foundation of the home where she grew up in rural Deaf Smith County, Texas. You can find it on my author page at Amazon.

She loved visits with Alan and Vickie's family from Haslet, Texas, and Ira's children and grandchildren from Lubbock.

As we concluded the family memoir, she chuckled over her five brother's antics, but her eyes often teared up when talking about what her mother endured while raising them through Papa's death, the Great Depression, and the Dust Bowl.

As I wrote, she was a stickler for the facts and wouldn't let me fictionalize a missing scene or someone's thoughts or feelings. After six years of writing and working with a group of other writers/editors, the book was published in December 2019. It is available on Amazon as a paperback or Kindle eBook.

Her descriptions in several of her scrapbooks helped her remember the stories of Africa. She loved that time and shared her gratitude for the work of the families she served there. She enjoyed seeing their children grow up and was thankful she played a tiny part in their growth.

She still hears from some missionaries, their families, and even the children she taught. She follows their ministries with great joy.

Connecting to the next generation is one of her goals and favorite activities. When her great-grandchildren came to town, she played "Go Fish" and "Trash" card games until her sight became too blurred.

Until 2020, Mom and I went everywhere together. Phill often joined us and called us the Three Musketeers. We enthusiastically participated in church, ladies' Bible class, and water aerobics. In 2020, my daughter Penelope came with her boys and dogs for a six-week stay. Mom enjoyed the full house.

Mom, at 99, loves restful breaks in her warm, golden lift chair near the pictures of her beloved Daddy Wilson, Grandma Lula, and her mother, Alta. Although Mom can no longer see clearly, she smiles as she talks about the precious memories of her people.

Macular degeneration has blurred her sight, but she knows the voices of her closest friends and children. She cannot read anymore, not even to correctly turn on the knobs on the stove. She cannot see the television but sits and joins in while the family watches. She enjoys the news and documentaries.

Although she has plenty, she's concerned about her bank account and asks us to read her bank statement regularly. She's also worried about whether she tithed her church contribution.

Nova still has some clarity of mind (which her mother lost at 80). She uses a walker to get around. But she is still full of the humor that suited her well and helped her cope with life's pitfalls.

On Palm Sunday of 2024, Mom suffered an "episode" of hallucinations and unconsciousness that made us feel she needed twenty-four-hour care. I did everything I could to keep her home, but nothing worked.

We searched for an assisted living or nursing facility and found one as close as possible to our current home. She seems to be doing better there and can have more independence. Ira, our families, and I visit her daily.

Recently, when Mom visited with Robin McCormack, her niece, Robin asked how Mom was doing. Mom responded, "Well, I think old age has finally caught up with me, but it's just temporary!" Yes, dear Mom, this life, with all its ups and downs, is temporary. If only we could all remember that.

Hers is not a defeated end. It is truly a gradual passing to a much more glorious life. Her balance has become unsteady, but her faith has not. Her eyesight is blurry, but her vision of eternity is sharp. She's sure she's landing "safe in the arms of Jesus," as the old hymn goes.

May we all age with such courage and humility. She lives her favorite hymn: "All the Way, My Savior Leads Me." "Heavenly peace, divinest comfort, here by faith in Him to dwell, for I know whate're befall me, Jesus doeth all things well."

Thank You, God, for giving me a mother with great joy, faithfulness, and love. Thank You for Grandma Wyly, who taught her children the ways of love early in their lives.

Dear Lord, You have led her steps in serving others. For many years, her life has been surrendered to Your kingdom and glory.

Mevanee Parmer
Amarillo, Texas

Nova's Thoughts on Ice Cream

"You can't buy happiness, but you can buy ice cream, ... and they're kind of the same thing."

Nova's Heart-Stopping Ice Cream Comment

Mom and I are very close. Once, as we chatted, we came to a serious moment in our discussion. She said quietly, "Well, just one thing before I die, I'm afraid . . ." She paused and looked at the floor. She did not complete the sentence.

My brain panicked and finished her thought 100 ways. "Maybe I've got siblings I don't know about. Did she accidentally steal millions of dollars? What confession am I about to hear that I never wanted to?"

I waited for several perilous seconds. Then, I prompted her, "You're afraid of what . . . exactly?

"I'm just afraid I won't ... (long pause) get enough ice cream before I die," she tried to suppress a chuckle.

"Whew!" I thought to myself, feeling I'd dodged a bullet. I replied with some consternation, "Mom, we can take care of that. You'll get enough ice cream."

Enigmatic, she has never suggested if another fear was behind the ice cream request. I now wonder if ice cream was really what was on her mind.

She does get enough ice cream. Every night, she gets the Nova Special Sundae. The recipe is simple, and she would want you to try it.

Two large scoops of Blue Bell Homemade Vanilla Ice Cream with a dash of buttermilk, chocolate syrup, and an Oreo Thin on top. (About the Oreo Thin: You must cut calories somewhere. The buttermilk adds a touch of tartness!) Celebrate Nova on your next ice-cream outing.

Saylor Sexton, one of my great-granddaughters, created this lovely cotton and paper portrait of me, one of my favorites! She noted, "If I live to be 120 years old, I would play card games."

Nova's Wonderful Hairdo

"Don't plan your funeral or wedding on Friday afternoon, or I won't be there. That's when I get my hair done." Nova's favorite hairdresser, Tricia Pope, asks Nova how she wants her hair fixed. Nova never has an answer, so Tricia always gives her the standard input, "Well, we'll make it cute and darlin'." So, Nova comes home "cute and darlin'" every time.

Ken could mend, fix, or restore almost anything. He kept cars running for all his children and grandchildren. And even rebuilt engines. He was a much-needed Mr. Fix It for Africa. Below he replaced a rotten board under my daughter's deck after the whole thing caved in. And he smiled as he worked.

A Tribute to Ken Vaughn

from Dell Purdy

I guess I was in about the 7th grade. My dad and I were driving home from a visit to my Grandma; we had gone over to her apartment to work on something because I was holding a socket set in my lap.

As we drove along, I turned to my dad, and with a quiver in my voice I said, "I'm not sure I want Grandma to go to Africa."

You see, she had recently retired and was planning to go to Kenya for an extended stay to help the mission team there. I think my dad might have been feeling the same fear and anxiety that I was because he responded by saying with a bit of a quiver in his voice, "Well, Dell, why don't you give her a call and talk with her about it?"

Now, before you judge us too harshly, let me say, I know we were on the wrong side of history on that one. But I was a boy who was worried about his grandma.

And as we drove along, my dad was a boy, worried about his mom. I got home and called Grandma. She listened to me and tried to calm my fears.

She said, "Dell, everything will be okay. This is something that I need to do. When I'm done, I'll come home and probably live out the rest of my life in Amarillo."

She went to Kenya and was blessed by the work there, and it wasn't too long after she came home that she started running around with Ken. We thought it was neat and kind of cute. Grandma has a boyfriend.

I remember the night that we found out that it was more than that. We were at Grandma's having dinner, and she had just gotten back from a visit with Mevanee and Phill for Thanksgiving. She told us that my cousin Shannon had asked if she and Ken were going to get married. We all chuckled, and then she said, "And I told her, 'I guess so.'"

As my mom recalls, we all froze mid-bite, our forks suspended in mid-air. We were surprised, and we didn't know what to make of it. Don't get me wrong, Ken seemed like a swell guy, but she was Grandma! Well, the plans were made, and they were married.

I can honestly say that Ken Vaughn has been one of the greatest blessings to my Grandma, our entire family, and me personally.

Some of the fondest memories of Ken are us working together on projects out in the garage. One weekend, Julie and I came up to Amarillo on a Sunday, and at lunch, I mentioned to Dad that my brakes were making some noise. Back at the house, Ken, Dad, and I dug into it, and sure enough, my brakes were worn down to metal on metal. The afternoon was spent working in the garage, running to the parts store, getting rotors turned. When we finally got done, we had to get on the road to head home.

I remember telling my grandma that I was sorry we hadn't been able to visit more; she said, "That's okay. Ken would rather be out there with you guys than sitting around visiting."

It was true, he loved to work, and it was great to work with Ken. He was a master mechanic and could figure out how to fix most anything. But as impressive as his skills were, the thing that set him apart was his gentle, patient, unflappable spirit when he worked. As skilled as Ken was, I was equally ham-handed. But I don't remember him ever being irritated with me, impatient, or frustrated in the least. He was fun to work with.

When I was in high school, my dad bought an old pickup for $100. The engine needed to be rebuilt, and Ken, Dad, and I worked together on it. When we were taking the motor apart, we were pulling off the head, and as we were taking the head bolts out, one of them broke.

If you've ever experienced a bolt breaking when you're trying to take it out, it's a terrible experience. We took the rest of the bolts out and removed the head, only to discover that it had broken off smoothly with the engine block and that there was nothing to grab on to get it out. The mood in the garage shifted. Deep sighs, the sound of wrenches hitting the concrete floor, frustration. But none of that was coming from Ken.

He went inside and asked for an ice pick. He came back out, took a hammer and that ice pick, and slowly, methodically started chipping away at that broken bolt. I don't remember how long it took, but it was a while. He chipped all that bolt out of the block, and he didn't damage the threads with a hammer and an ice pick.

I don't know if you know this, but ice picks aren't designed to chip out steel bolts. Even more impressive, after hours working on that, he hadn't bent the ice pick, and he hadn't cracked the handle. He didn't break it. I can't tell you how many times I've broken a tool using it for the job it was designed to do, but Ken didn't break an ice pick while chipping away at a metal bolt. He didn't break it. But he had worn it down from about 6 inches to about 2 inches over a few hours.

That memory means a lot to me. And you might think it's funny to share a story about working on a pickup at a memorial service, but I think it says something about the way he worked and the way he lived. I've told that story to people before, and they say, "Well, why didn't he use this or that, or do x, y, z." I don't know the answers to those questions, but I guess it's because we didn't have "this or that, or x, y, z." We had an ice pick, a hammer, and time. So, Ken took what we had, and he got the job done.

And Ken loved to talk and tell stories. I remember not long after Grandma and Ken had married, my friend and I were over at their house working on something at the kitchen table. Ken came and sat with us and told us, "My neighbor had one of those Chihuahua dogs...those dogs, they don't have much hair." And that was the end of the story. And we loved it!

Ken was easy to talk to, and I loved listening to him. I loved hearing stories about his work at Sears or in the Mechanic's shop. Because of his skill and temperament, he would often get weird problems that no one else could figure out. Like the car with the gas gauge that would go crazy every time you turned a corner that turned out to be a yo-yo tied to the float by a practical joker in the factory.

I loved hearing about the things he saw on his trips to Kenya and Uganda, about the ways that construction was done, and about a few resourceful guys on the side of the road that had managed to pull the engine out of their truck and rebuild it using only a few hand tools. I loved listening to him talk and tell stories. And there were many of his stories that I'd heard more than once, but I didn't mind.

A few months ago, we were here visiting Ken and Grandma. Ken didn't have much strength and spent most of his time in the recliner by that time. The kids were playing in the backyard, and I went to sit on the porch. After a few minutes, Ken came out and sat by me. As we sat together, I started asking leading questions, hoping to hear some of his stories again…but he was tired. His breathing was heavy, and he didn't say much.

As we sat there, I just wanted to hear his stories again. I know that Ken is far better today than he was before. But selfishly, I wish for one more time sitting with him, listening to his stories, one more project with his wisdom and skillful hand to guide. I love Ken, and I will be forever grateful for his influence on my life and the blessing that he has been to my Grandma and our family.

Sometimes I think our images of Heaven are pretty weak. Images of chubby babies with wings sitting on clouds playing harps. It's hard to imagine a man like Ken, who loved to work, being in heaven in a place like that.

But I think it's important to remember that when we meet God in scripture, we first see him creating, doing work, and preparing a place for Adam to live. I'm also reminded of a time when Jesus' disciples were anxious about a future where he would not be with them in person, and he said to them, "Do not let your hearts be troubled. Trust in God; trust also in me. In my Father's house are many rooms; if it were not so, I would have told you. I am going there to *prepare* a place for you. And if I go and *prepare* a place for you, I will come back and take you to be with me that you also may be where I am."

It strikes me that Jesus talks about preparation being done in heaven, work being done in heaven. I can't help but wonder if Ken isn't a part of that work today. He is working hard with strong hands, with a strong heart and healthy body, doing what he always has done, working hard, using his skills and strengths to the glory of God.

Nova's Thoughts on Aging and Dying

I believe in the hereafter. I'm always going into a room and saying, "What am I here after?"

As I (Mevanee) am rubbing my mother's aching right shoulder, she tells me, "I want to go home to the Lord now! I don't know what the hold-up is." The date is December 2021.

I suggest, "The line is long right now with all the COVID deaths, and we have to wait our turn. It's an administrative backlog. Or maybe it's like Shannon (Nova's granddaughter) teases, 'The Lord is giving **you** time to repent.'"

"Or," Nova suggests, "The Lord is trying to teach **you** a lesson by leaving **me** here."

"Yes," I reply, "and if **I** hurried up and learned it, **you** could go on home. Or maybe the Lord wants **me** to die first so I can take care of **you** in heaven."

"Well, who will take care of Phill (my husband) if you're not around?" she queries.

"His second wife," I reply immediately, "who will be more kind and patient than I am."

"Oh, so there is a long line of kind and patient women somewhere? Are you sure?" She sounds dubious.

"Come to think of it, maybe not a long line. That sounds like a future chapter in the series of novels, *The #1 Ladies Detective Agency*, 'The Long Line of Kind and Patient Women.'" (We have read all the Mama Ramotswe series by Alexander McCall Smith, so she understands the allusion.)

As Nova enjoys her nightly ice cream sundae, she quips a little sadly, "All my health nut friends are dead."

Acknowledgments

Many thanks to my proofreaders, Patsy Rae Dawson and Janelle Perdue Hulsey of the Truth Tellers critique group in Amarillo, Texas. Thank you, Patsy, for coming up with the sweetly humorous title for the book. Working with both of you has convinced me of the power of the personal memoir! Your help with the typesetting and details was immeasurable. I wouldn't have made it without you.

Thank you to Shelly Schmidt, a dear friend and professor at the University of Illinois, Champaign, who volunteered time from her busy schedule to proofread. Phill Parmer, Nova's favorite son-in-law (in her own words), is our expert editor-in-residence and encourager.

Thank you, Penelope, my daughter who insisted on editing while restarting her career. Shannon's questions and weekly pep rally for my work always encouraged me. I am so grateful for edits, guiding comments, encouragements, and queries. I'm grateful to my son, Cory, for helping arrange the family outing which refreshed my heart and soul.

We are grateful to Dell Purdy for his tribute to Ken Vaughn, or KenPa, as his stepchildren and grandchildren called him. Your example of Ken's patience remains in my heart and will be there forever.

Steven Arias is a great book cover designer at Sir Speedy in Amarillo. I appreciate his work.

And to sweet Samantha Wyly and S&S Photography for working us into their busy schedule. We love your family portraits.

Thank you to Saylor Sexton, one of Nova's granddaughters, for creating an apt portrait of Nova on page 108 and letting us share it.

I am thankful for my siblings, Ira and Alan, and their spouses, Linda and Vickie, respectively, Nova's grandchildren and great-grandchildren, and Ken's family. Nova loves each of you. Your interaction with her has made her life rich and satisfying. She's enjoyed the many ways you have held up her hands.

We are grateful for the faith families where Ken and Nova have ministered and been loved. Given Nova's failing memory, we do not know how many churches they've visited. God has the true record of all their lives. Their most recent church family is Central Church of Christ in Amarillo, Texas.

In Ken's last months, he repeated his conversion story over and over. Finding the Church of Christ was the most significant change in his life as a young man.

A radio program beamed to rural Alabama led him to seek out a church in Birmingham, where he was welcomed and transformed. Ken and Nova first met at a Bible Reading in Fort Worth. The church has been a formative force for good for Nova all her life.

Nova Vaughn is a wonderfully straightforward person. Her attitude about life is simple but not easy. She is so full of integrity and kindness that she supposes most people are like she is. May they be so! She has shared with several women's groups in the United States and Africa. And might be available for a cup of tea if you are in Amarillo.

Mevanee Parmer is passionate about sharing the voices of her High Plains ancestors and relatives. She is the editor of the survival story and memoir **Keep on the Sunny Side,** detailing the faith and heroism of her grandmother, Alta Wyly. She has also published short stories and poetry in **With Words We Weave,** an anthology published by the Texas High Plains Writers. Her writing reflects her Texas roots.

Keep on the Sunny Side

Keep on the Sunny Side reveals the walk of faith of Alta Wilson Wyly, a settler of the Texas Panhandle. Over 100 vintage photographs, paintings, journal entries, and poems tell her story of inspiration and courage.

She and her husband, Jim, bought land in Deaf Smith County, Texas, in 1927. By 1929, they had a bumper wheat crop. Jim died in a tragic accident that fall, yet Alta managed her resources and emotions to keep her children on their farm through the Great Depression, the Dust Bowl, and beyond.

Learn her secrets of survival and her humor as she nurtured her seven children through the Dirty Thirties. Her mother and grandmother's faith strengthened her, and she inspires readers to find their strength in God.

Excerpts from her diaries, letters, and accounts given by her children and grandchildren allow the reader to experience the saga of her heroism. Alta's labors as a widow raising seven children resonate with many who settled and farmed in the Panhandle of Texas from 1929 through the 1950s.

Keep on the Sunny Side is available on Amazon as a paperback or Kindle Book.

Made in the USA
Monee, IL
26 November 2024